Runes

In Focus

Runes

In Focus

Jan Budkowski

ZAMBEZI PUBLISHING LTD
www.zampub.com

First published in 2016 in the UK by Zambezi Publishing Ltd
Plymouth, Devon PL2 2EQ
Tel: +44 (0)1752 367 300   Fax: +44 (0)1752 350 453
email: info@zampub.com   www.zampub.com

British Library Cataloguing in Publication Data:
A catalogue record for this book is available from the British Library
ISBN: 978-1-903065-19-8
Illustrations copyright © 2016 Jan Budkowski,
Adobe Stock Images and others
Typesetting by Zambezi Publishing Ltd, Plymouth
Printed in the UK by Lightning Source UK

About the Author

Jan was born in Lusaka in Zambia, and after a happy childhood and good education, he took a job in banking. Over time, he worked his way up to an executive position and spent thirty one years in banking. However, Jan was also into psychology, astrology and ancient mythology. These interests led him to an interest in the Runes and the way that they can be used for counselling or forecasting purposes.

Later, Jan realised that there was more to life than the financial arena, and at the same time, he came to the UK and turned to writing and then to publishing, together with his wife, Sasha Fenton. Jan has written three previous books and several articles, as well as occasional radio broadcasts on financial and mind, body and spirit matters. He lives and works in Devon with Sasha, In his spare time, he loves golf, fly fishing, archery and photography.

Previous books:
Dreams
Prophecy for Profit
The Money Book

Contents

Introducing the Runes 3

1: Where did the Runes come from? 19

2: The Story of Odin 25

3: Yggdrasil - the World Tree of Life 29

4: Background to the Norse Gods and Goddesses .33

5: The Nine Worlds 37

6: Symbols of the Runes .41

7: Making or Buying your Runes 43

8: Freya's Aett 47

9: Hagal's Aett 63

10: Tyr's Aett 77

11: Preparing a New Set of Runes 95

12: Before you Read your Runes 97

13: Reading the Runes 101

14: Larger Spreads 105

15: The Compass Layout .111

16: Crossover Layouts 117

17: Magic with the Runes .125

18: Initial Letters 127

19: Pronunciation 133

Conclusion 137

Index 139

INTRODUCING THE RUNES

What is a Rune?
A Rune is a symbol for a letter of the Norse alphabet, but the word also means something secret and mysterious.

What is in This Book?
In this book, I talk about the mythology behind each Rune, but I also describe the meaning of each for predictive purposes. A Rune reading can throw light on a murky situation, and it can offer advice as to the best way forward. It can also predict the trends and events that are due to come into being.

Right from the first moment of their existence, the Runes have been used for magical purposes, so if you put a Rune or two on your altar when spellcasting, you are following an ancient tradition. The same goes for when you use them to divine the future.

By describing the legends associated with the Norse gods, I show how their beliefs gave meaning to the Runes. Unlike the tarot, playing cards or even chess, Runes do not reflect the lives of kings, queens and courtiers, because they focus on the lives of the Norse and Saxon people who worked on the land, fished and travelled from one place to another to buy and sell their produce. In short, the Runes were always about ordinary people and they still are, which is why they still offer down to earth messages that make sense to all of us today.

So now, you can discover how to make your own Runes if you wish to do so, and you can delve into the meaning of each Rune, and see examples of spreads that you can use for Rune reading.

Important Note
I give the upright and reversed interpretations in this book, but you can read the Runes as if they were upright only, if you prefer.

The full set of Norse Runes

The common name for the twenty-four Runes in the northern set is the Futhark, a name derived from the first six Runes. The Runes are divided into three sub-sets, each dedicated to Freya, Hagal and Tyr; these are the goddess and two gods respectively from the Aesir pantheon.

For ease of reference, these three subsets – Freya's Aett, Hagal's Aett and Tyr's Aett – are shown below.

FREYA'S AETT			
1 Fehu	2 Uruz	3 Thurisaz	4 Ansuz
5 Raido	6 Kaunaz	7 Gebo	8 Wunjo
HAGAL'S AETT			
9 Hagalaz	10 Nauthiz	11 Isa	12 Jera
13 Eihwaz	14 Pertho	15 Algiz	16 Sowelo
TYR'S AETT			
17 Tiwaz	18 Berkano	19 Ehwaz	20 Mannaz
21 Laguz	22 Inguz	23 Othila	24 Dagaz

ᚠ	ᚢ	ᚦ	ᚨ
Fehu	Uruz	Thurisaz	Ansuz
ᚱ	ᚲ	ᚷ	ᚹ
Raido	Kaunaz	Gebo	Wunjo
ᚺ	ᚾ	ᛁ	ᛃ
Hagalaz	Nauthiz	Isa	Jera
ᛇ	ᛈ	ᛉ	ᛊ
Eihwaz	Pertho	Algiz	Sowelo
ᛏ	ᛒ	ᛗ	ᛘ
Tiwaz	Berkano	Ehwaz	Mannaz
ᛚ	ᛜ	ᛟ	ᛞ
Laguz	Inguz	Othila	Dagaz

The Runes

Ritual and invocation

The best Runes are always those that you make for yourself. It is traditional before beginning this task to make a dedication to Odin, the ruler of the Norse gods. Legend tells us that Odin hung himself upside down from the sacred tree, Yggdrasil, and he stayed like this for nine days and nights. During this time, he reached enlightenment, and then he found the Runes among the roots of the tree. Odin is associated with communication, intellect, logic, travel, healing and divination.

You can begin by burning some incense, such as mastic gum or tiny strips of hazel wood. Make an invocation to Odin and visualize the god himself while speaking aloud. He has only one eye and he hides the empty socket under the brim of a large hat. He also wears a cloak, carries a blackthorn staff and is accompanied by a raven. Odin rides the magical, eight-legged horse, Sleipnir, on whose back Odin travels between the Nine Worlds.

An Invocation to Odin
(by Seldiy Bate, Summer Solstice, 1987)

Lord of the Northern Wind, by Sea and Sky,
By Baldur's burning Sun and Freya's Moon,
I call upon thee, O Mighty Odin, that I
May learn the secret of each and every Rune!
I have worked the magicks well, and poured
a libation of mead by the trembling blackthorn tree,
have listened to the Raven's voice and scored
My name upon a Hazel wand for thee;
For he that calls the Divine King Odin and proves
Himself to be worthy of the wisdom will hear
the eightfold drumming of Sleipnir's flashing hooves
And know the wisest of the gods is near.
A gift demands a gift, Grim Guardian of Death
Whisper'd secrets on Odin's sacred breath!

Rune Meanings in Brief

The Rune set is sometimes called the FUTHARK after the first six letters of the Runic alphabet. (Fehu, Uruz, Thurisaz, Ansuz, Raido, Kaunaz).

The twenty-four Runes are split into three sets, each dedicated to Freya, Hagall and Tyr respectively, and the complete set is sometimes referred to as the *Aettir*.

Runic letter   : **FEHU**
English equivalent : **F**
Keyword   : **Cattle**
Cattle represented prosperity or wealth in the ancient world, much as they do in parts of Africa today. So, this Rune represents the querent's personal property and funds, his wealth, career status and position. Fehu represents material security, sometimes also emotional security and if appropriate, pregnancy, as well as fertility and growth of all kinds.

If reversed, it can indicate financial loss and a lack of fulfilment, female health problems, an inability to become pregnant, and obesity.

Runic letter   : **URUZ**
English equivalent : **U or W**
Keyword   : **Wild Ox**
The powerful ox represents masculinity, the active principle and the physical and material planes. This brings opportunities, possibly a financial improvement, but always with the expenditure of energy or strength. This can mean learning or teaching, particularly some kind of physical skill.

If reversed, this can suggest missed opportunities, physical or moral weakness or outbursts of anger.

Runic letter   : **THURISAZ**
English equivalent   : **TH**
Keyword   : **A thorn**

Thurisaz can denote protection from attack, and even the use of an offensive deterrent if other Runes nearby indicate this. This can also mean jumping to the defence of others. Decisions will require a certain element of caution and perhaps self-protection as well. The querent must allow matters to run their course and not rush into anything. There may be something in the house or within the family that needs attention.

When reversed, Thurisaz denotes defensiveness, anger or bullying, or being on the receiving end of this kind of thing.

Runic letter   : **ANSUZ**
English equivalent   : **A or O**
Keyword   : **A god**

This Rune is sacred to Odin, so it represents authority, superiors, elders and ancestors, father figures or god figures in the querent's life. This can also apply to the querent's spiritual progress, beliefs and philosophy, and it can denote guidance from above.

Reversed, it suggests problems with older people, authority figures, the authorities and possibly throwing one's weight around. It can indicate a fanatical or obsessive outlook.

Runic letter   : **RAIDO**
English equivalent   : **R**
Keyword   : **A wheel**

This Rune suggests a journey with a purpose. This includes transport matters and all kinds of physical movement and exploration, but also mental travel, such as studying and using one's imagination. It brings change, the turning of events and progress , even if this means reviving something that has been left for a while.

Reversed, this Rune brings difficulties related to vehicles and transport, a stubborn refusal to change, or rushing into something without thinking it through properly.

Runic letter : KAUNAZ
English equivalent : K or a hard C
Keyword : A bonfire

Health, wealth, status and reputation are all on the way up now, while social life also picks up. It can also suggest great ideas or a burst of creative energy. This Rune is especially lucky for a woman, as she can expect to receive love from a man, whilst a male would find himself in the position of giving love. This may indicate the kindling of a new relationship.

Reversed, this Rune brings loss, sadness and increasingly bad health. Something valuable may be lost.

Runic letter : GEBO
English equivalent : G
Keyword : A gift

This Rune may bring a gift, a contract or an opportunity, and it suggests that the individual has some kind of useful gift or talent. This also brings beneficial partnerships and happiness in love, but it implies that "give and take" must be part of the relationship. In Runic lore, we are never given anything for nothing, so we must be prepared to pay in some way for whatever we receive.

The reversed meaning makes it hard for the person to get on in life. He may lack a specific qualification or ability, which makes it hard for him to get the right kind of job. Sickness or wasted effort may also apply.

Runic letter   : WUNJO
English equivalent : W or U
Keyword   : Joy

This Rune brings joy and happiness, but it is associated with water, and therefore it suggests a journey over water, or perhaps a home near water. Alternatively, an important visitor could come from over the water. There may be an artistic or spiritual awakening and there may also be gain or luck in respect of creative or inspirational matters. Sometimes this Rune foretells the appearance of a fair-haired man.

When reversed, Wunjo indicates stress, difficulties and depression, but it can also denote health problems related to menstruation or body fluids. There is difficulty in seeing clearly, and also bad judgment. Wunjo reversed often suggests the need to wait three months before making a decision that is directly related to an emotional matter, or three days before making a work-related decision.

Runic letter   : HAGALAZ
English equivalent : H
Keyword   : Hail

Hagalaz implies havoc, disruption of plans and unforeseen events. Even good events are possible, but they might turn the person's world upside down. There may be illness in the family or unexpected and unwanted pregnancies, but even if there is destruction, this allows the subject to rebuild in a better way. It is even possible that the disaster is self-inflicted. Sometimes this Rune warns of a death, but only if other Runes near it emphasise this possibility.

It is not possible to give an inverted meaning to Hagalaz, as the Rune means the same either way up.

Runic letter   : NAUTHIZ
English equivalent : N
Keyword   : Need

This Rune is associated with necessity, self-preservation and natural, instinctive requirements such as the need for food, shelter and to protect one's children - even perhaps to save one's own skin. This Rune also rules such needs as creativity and the need for a job or a relationship. The motivating force is the need to function and to achieve. There is also a warning here to be patient and to exercise restraint.

Reversed, it can represent tightened muscles and aching limbs, but also a rigid and uptight personality, who can't let go of resentment and anger.

Runic letter   : ISA
English equivalent : I
Keyword   : Ice

Plans may be halted, money may be immobilized and nothing good can come of the present situation, so the instruction here is to leave things alone and to try again another time. Feelings might be frozen and the individual may no longer care about people or situations that have had their day. This is like the ice of winter that always melts in the spring, so there will be warmth and growth in time, but patience is needed.

When reversed, there may be fear, immobilisation in the person's affairs and loneliness. There could be some physical impediment, such as rheumatism or paralysis. Perhaps there is immobility or mental paralysis with no clear or constructive ideas, in addition to obstinacy and a refusal to adapt.

Runic letter   : JERA
English equivalent : Y or soft G
Keyword   : Cycle or harvest

This is like the turning of the seasons or the wheel of fortune. There may be a waiting period, a time of expectation and a promise of fulfilment. The querent will reap what has been sown for good or for ill. This is a time to pay debts, to make a start on new projects, to sign contracts and perhaps even to move house. In other words, this is the time for a fresh start, possibly with the help of others.

The reversed Rune is similar, although the person may miss out on something if he or she refuses to adapt to a new situation. It may take a year for the situation to resolve itself.

Runic letter   : EIHWAZ
English equivalent : EI (as in rise)
Keyword   : Yew bow

The yew bow is flexible enough to adapt itself to a new shape without breaking; therefore, this suggests a kind of recoiling, retreating or stepping out of the way of difficulty. The querent will have to take a flexible approach to life and adapt himself to a new and different situation. He may even take one step backward in order to move two steps forwards. Pitfalls will be avoided, and inconvenient situations will turn out advantageous in the end. The querent may be able to use the strength of others against them (as in some martial arts), or to avoid the manipulative behaviour of others or their dominance in order to find another way around a problem. He will need to do some lateral thinking.

If Eithwaz is reversed, the person may be indecisive, or apt to switch from one thing to another. He may suffer from the bad behaviour of others, especially those who are sly and devious. He may become weak or even temporarily mentally ill, or he may not want to face up to things.

Runic letter   : PERTHO
English equivalent : P
Keyword   : The secret Rune

If this is the first Rune to appear in a reading, it might be better to leave it and try again a few days or even a few weeks later. It suggests a link with the spirit world, psychism, dreams, visions and trance-like states, but it may also mean that something is hidden from view and has yet to come to light. Pertho indicates unexpectedly good events, luck, abundance and the return of favours about which the querent may have forgotten.

It can bring unexpected bounty, but when reversed, it foretells a time of worry and fear or disappointment. Also, something may be going on behind the subject's back.

Runic letter   : ALGIZ
English equivalent : E or Y
Keyword   : A hand, upright in greeting. A reed

This Rune has connections with the reed in a musical instrument, in that it suggests artistry, poetry and creative talent or self-expression, so it denotes hobbies, cultural interests and study for pleasure. It can also mean belonging to a special group that uses its own behaviour and vocabulary.

The reversed Rune suggests that the subject should choose his friends with care and stay away from bad influences. He may find it hard to be creative at the moment.

Runic letter   : SOWELO
English equivalent : S
Keyword   : The sun

Sowelo represents the life force, health and healing, but also rest and recuperation. It rules relaxation and activities such as sport, hobbies, vacations and entertainment. On other levels, it can indicate success, fame, recognition and bringing a creative endeavour or talent out into the light.

When Sowelo is reversed, it simply means that the person should relax, have some fun and give himself time to rest.

Runic letter   : TIWAZ
English equivalent   : T
Keyword   : The war god

This Rune implies activity, energy and heroism. A male querent will soon seek romance, while a female will soon find a new lover or partner. Any ensuing romance would be full of passion and overwhelming feelings. There may also be anger, aggression, angst and even the need to go on the attack.

When Tiwaz is reversed, there may be a lack of energy. For a male querent, a broken love affair or unrequited love, possibly caused by being too pushy. For a female, possibly falling for the wrong person or an obsessive relationship. Other possibilities are sexual frustration, impotence, arguments, accidents and illness.

Runic letter   : BERKANO
English equivalent   : B
Keyword   : Birch tree

Berkano is associated with fertility cults and pagan rituals, springtime and the awakening of the life force. Therefore, this Rune can mean new beginnings, expansion, celebrations, weddings and births. It represents joy in the family, but also ritual, familiarity and repetition or routine.

When reversed, it means illness in the family, disconcerting visits, unfamiliar surroundings, and bad news in the community or ill feeling among friends. Things that are delayed, fatigue and lassitude.

Runic letter : EHWAZ
English equivalent : E (as in day)
Keyword : Horse

This relates to travel and transport, movement and methods of transport such as the querent's car, the bus that he takes or even his feet. On a working farm, this relates to animals but it can also signify pets. This Rune is concerned with change, and the methods that are used to bring it about, in addition to ideas and the medium that is used to put them across to others. This is related to all forms of communication and progress, and how it is achieved.

Reversed, this Rune means problems with transport and delays. Sick animals feature here, as do ill people, immobility and handicaps. Also, failure to get a message across, or the wrong approach.

Runic letter : MANNAZ
English equivalent : M
Keyword : Man

A male figure, a man in authority or a professional man is indicated. The Rune tells the querent not to forge ahead with any project without consulting a professional person.

Reversed, Maunaz means that there may be problems with authority figures, differences of opinion or disagreements with father figures, bosses or even foreigners.

Runic letter : LAGUZ
English equivalent : L
Keyword : Lake

Laguz can indicate a woman in a reading - although she has to be of an age and type who is capable of giving birth, as the Rune also rules fertility and children. This rules the unknown and the universal world of the spirit rather than personal affairs. This is a feminine Rune, connected to the moon goddess, the sea, the psychic realms, intuition and the mysteries of childbirth. This symbolizes anything that allows change and fluidity. It also applies to protection and a kind of womb-like safety.

When Laguz is reversed, there could be female health problems, escapism and even alcohol or drug dependence.

Runic letter   : INGUZ
English equivalent   : NG
Keyword   : The Danes

The idea here is that something is going on that produces a result or completes a project, and this can apply to long-term projects or problem solving. It also suggests protection; enclosure, security and staying put in familiar surroundings. This Rune can refer to friends - particularly if they are from overseas. It is also associated with magic, divination and women's mysteries by an association with the mother goddess.

Reversed, Inguz can indicate health issues, stress and restriction. It will be hard to produce or achieve anything.

Runic letter   : OTHILA
English equivalent   : E or O
Keyword   : Inheritance

This denotes benefit through property, gifts and help from older relatives, also inheritance, heirlooms and an actual object that is left to the querent. It is also associated with documents, wills, legal matters and anything related to money.

When reversed, it can disrupt the family, bring sudden change and force the person to let go of outdated ideas.

Runic letter	: DAGAZ
English equivalent	: D
Keyword	: Day

Daytime, warmth and light are indicated, so the Rune refers to anything that is open, obvious and easily seen. If this is close to the blank Rune, success is a matter of fate or destiny. It may be worth setting an appropriate date for something to happen, making relevant preparations and then waiting for it to come around. It can indicate advertisement, image, clarity and recognition. Also success in studies, passing tests and gaining qualifications, a change for the better and success in general.

This Rune doesn't change its meaning when reversed, other than to suggest that something has yet to be revealed. At worst, this can imply a need for sleep and a period under anaesthetic, or in a coma.

The Blank Rune - Wyrd

| Keyword: | Destiny, fate. |

The Blank Rune is associated with fate and anything else that is out of the questioner's own hands, or matters that are only known to the gods. Look at the Runes that are nearby to see what the fates have in store.

1: Where did the Runes come from?

We tend to think of the Runes as a Nordic or north German invention, but their beginnings can be traced to ancient Greece and then to northern Italy and the Etruscans, spreading ever northwards via the major river routes. Some of the earliest forms of runic writing developed in Bohemia, which is the modern-day Czech Republic and Slovakia, but in time, they reached the north German lands and Scandinavia.

Over time, Latin became the main written language of Europe, and the Latin lettering that we still use today became the norm. However, the Romans never managed to subdue northern Europe, so runic writing clung on in those lands. Nordic mythology and the Runes themselves lost ground when Christianity took hold, but the less Christianised Icelanders wrote down the myths and kept the ancient forms of writing alive. There were still some Runes in use in Britain even in medieval times, but they gradually fell out of use once printing started the process of standardising written English.

Runic lettering changed over time, partly due to the fact that early Runes were carved and etched into wood and stone, and later, impressed into pottery or written down.

Writing at the end of the first century AD, the Roman historian *Tacitus* described the Teutonic peoples in his work called *Germania*. He was mainly interested in the tribes to the north of the Alps detailing their social customs, physical appearance and aggressive tendencies. Usefully, he also was the first to describe the use of Runes as a divinatory tool.

The word "Rune" means a secret thing, or something mysterious. Secret talks were called "Ruenes", and the fourth century Bishop Wulfila used the word "Runa" to mean mystery. The early Germanic word "Raunen" means "whisper".

So, right from the start, the mysterious Runes were both a form of writing and a means of conveying magical and mystical energies from one place to another.

A Quote from Tacitus' Tome, Germania:

"No people practise augury and divination by lot more diligently. The use of the lots is simple; a little bough is lopped off a fruit-bearing tree and cut into small pieces: these are distinguished by certain marks, and thrown carelessly at random over a white garment.
In public, the priest of the particular state, in private the father of the family, invokes the gods, and with his eyes towards heaven, takes up each piece three times, and finds in them a meaning according to the mark previously impressed upon them. If they prove unfavourable, there is no further consultation that day about the matter."

We should look more closely at the social and religious environment of the original Germanic peoples, otherwise a full understanding of the Runes is difficult. In his book, *Germania*, Tacitus recorded a succinct overview of the deities that these people worshipped. Enlisting the Roman equivalent names, he described similarities to Isis, Mars, Hercules and Mercury. Frigga was likened to Isis. Tyr or Tiwaz was linked to Mars, the Roman god of war, while Hercules was easily seen as Thor, with his magical hammer. Mercury, the god of commerce, divination and travel had attributes similar to Odin / Wotan. We should be really grateful to Tacitus, as the historical records he left us have given us a very thorough insight into the Germanic tribes of those times. However, my book only has space for an overview of all the absorbing details.

Turning to the more northern tales and religions connected to the Runes, we look towards Iceland and the epic poems and sagas that have survived through the centuries from medieval times to this day. A family tree of the main gods, goddesses and associated magical characters is illustrated here:

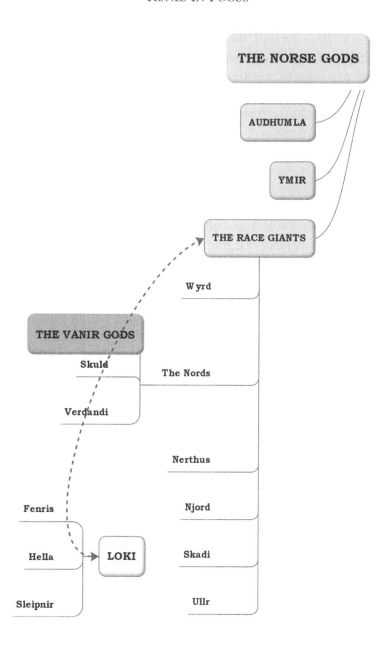

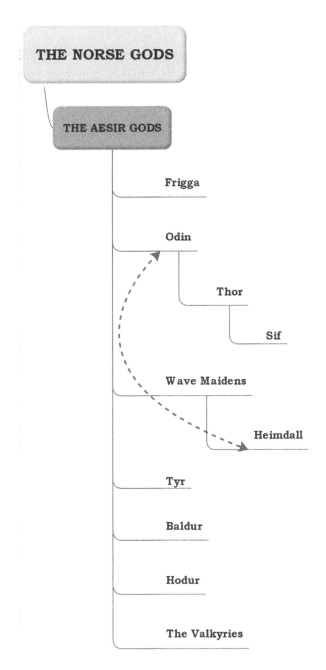

THE NORSE GODS

THE AESIR GODS

Frigga

Odin

Thor

Sif

Wave Maidens

Heimdall

Tyr

Baldur

Hodur

The Valkyries

The Gods and the Runes

The gods and their domains are often associated with certain Runes, but not all the gods have a Rune, whereas some gods have several Runes to their names.

GOD	RUNE
Audhumla	Fehu
Ymir	Uruz
The Race Giants	Thurisaz
Wyrd	The blank Rune
The Norns	All the Runes
Urd	Hagalaz
Skuld	Nauthiz
Verdani	Isa
Loki	Kaunaz, Jera, Dagaz
Nerthus	Laguz
Njord	Laguz
Skadi	—
Ullr	Eihwaz
Fenris	Tiwaz
Hella	Hagalaz
Sleipnir	Ehwaz
Frigga	Wunjo, Pertho, Berkano
Odin	Ansuz, Gebo, Othila
Wave Maidens	—
Thor	Uruz, Thurisaz, Gebo, Sowelo
Sif	—
Heimdall	Kaunaz, Hagalaz, Algiz, Dagaz, Mannaz
Tyr	Tiwaz
Baldur	Jera, Sowelo
Hodur	Jera, Sowelo
The Valkyries	Algiz

2: THE STORY OF ODIN

Odin's Sacrifice

A terrible war arose between the two branches of the gods, the Vanir and the Aesir. Won by the Vanir as a result of their ability to foresee the future, Odin vowed to balance the odds for any future conflict. After the war, peace ensued, with an exchange of hostages in order to prevent any future clashes. Njord and his two children, Frey and Freya, moved to Odin's dominion of Asgard, while Odin's brother Hoenir switched abode to Vanaheim, the home of the Vanir.

Subsequently, Odin voluntarily endured a dreadful ordeal in order to gain understanding and mastery of the Runes, but more about that later on.

Translations abound of the Rune Poem of the Poetic Edda and the Rúnatal, the stanzas of the Havamal tale that describe Odin's painful test of endurance – some more poetic and imaginative than others. Because so many scholarly versions differ significantly from each other, here is my compilation of the episode, in what I consider the most likely expression of the original:

Odin's Poem
"Wounded I hung on a wind-swept gallows
For nine long nights,
Pierced by a spear, pledged to Odhinn,
Offered myself to myself,
The wisest know not whence spring
The roots of that ancient rood.
No bread did they give me nor a drink from a horn;
downwards I peered,
I took up the Runes, screaming I took them,
then I fell back from there."

A very expressive account by Odin himself; being the "godfather" of the gods, the highest offering he could make was, of course, to himself. He hung from a branch (poetically considered a gallows) of Yggdrasil, the ancient World Tree, burdened with a wound from his own spear, and already afflicted by having earlier given away his left eye in exchange for the universal wisdom that he sought.

Still feeling dissatisfied with the knowledge and skills he had now acquired, Odin visited Freya, the Vanir goddess and managed to persuade her to teach him skills in magic. Finally, Odin felt satisfied that he had earned the right to rule wisely as the king of the gods. Sadly, the Norse legends allowed their gods less than eternal lives, as their end was to happen in the tragic time of destruction that the Norse myths called Ragnarok. Odin could not alter that future, even with the help of the Runes.

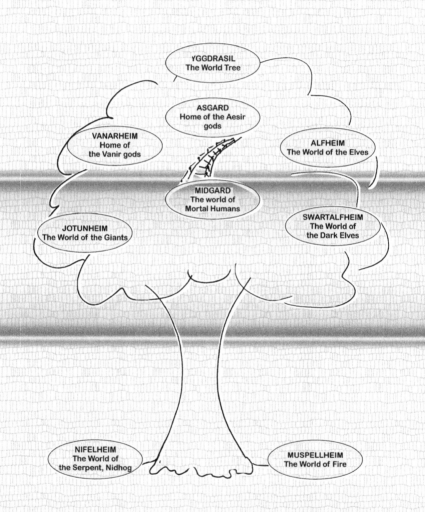

3:
YGGDRASIL - THE WORLD TREE OF LIFE

"There stands an ash called Yggdrasil,
A mighty tree showered in white hail.
From there come the dews that fall in the valleys.
It stands evergreen above Urd's Well.
From there come maidens, very wise,
Three from the lake that stands beneath the pole.
One is called Urd, another Verdandi,
Skuld the third; they carve into the tree
the lives and destinies of children."

FROM THE INSIGHT OF THE SEERESS VOLVA, FROM THE VOLUSPA (PROPHECY OF VOLVA) IN THE POETIC EDDA

The tree, Yggdrasil, grows out of the well of Urd. Urd, or Wyrd, means destiny, and the tree is said to hold the nine worlds in its branches. According to the ancient Norse myths, various creatures live in the tree, including Odin's eight-legged horse, Sleipnir, which rides up, down and across the tree, crossing from one world to the next and back again.

Even in ancient times, Yggdrasil and the gods were considered to be a hangover from the past, while even the ancients knew that life had to be lived in the present. One way to influence the present and the future was by the use of magic, and the Runes were used to focus the forces of destiny in such a way as to bring about the desired outcome.

Yggdrasil has three roots, the first of which becomes Asgard, home of Odin and his coterie of gods. The second leads to Jotunheim, the land of the giants, while the third leads to a hellish place called Niflheim, the mist world.

4: Background to the Norse Gods and Goddesses

The Norse Gods and Goddesses

The Norns / the Three Sisters

The Norns, goddesses of fate, are reputed to have created the runic alphabet. They were not allied to either the Aesir or the Vanir, though they apparently had some inclination to the Vanir. Owing allegiance to no one and beholden only to their mother, Wyrd, the Norns represented time in its entirety – past, present and future:

Urd, the eldest, represented the past

Verdandi, the young and lively Norn of the present, and

Skuld, veiled and holding an unopened document, was mistress of the future.

Tempestuous Skuld would often unwind the intricate plans of the other two Norns, thus confirming the vagaries and uncertainties of times to come.

The three sisters lived amongst the roots of Yggdrasil, and one of their duties was to water the tree from the well of Urd, thus ensuring the consistent development of Yggdrasil. Their main task, however, was to weave the web that directed the lives of humans and gods alike. The complexity of their web was such that no one could see both the start and ending of the massive, living web.

It is most likely that the Norns were the inspiration for future fables, ranging from Sleeping Beauty's three good fairies to Shakespeare's three witches in Macbeth, and the neo-pagan goddesses called the crone, mother and maiden.

Vanir and Aesir

The two main divisions of gods in the Norse pantheon were the Aesir and the Vanir.

The Aesir

Ruled by Odin, the Aesir included Odin's wife Frigga, along with Thor, Tyr, Baldur, and Hodur. The Rainbow Bridge that linked heaven and earth was guarded by Heimdall, one of Odin's extra-marital progeny, awesomely enough through his dalliance with the Wave Maidens; these nine sea giantesses somehow all managed to be Heimdall's mother. Such feats, no doubt, were simply beyond mere mortal comprehension!

As we occasionally find the traditional black sheep in families nowadays, the Aesir had in their midst Loki, the god of wild and raging fire; the direct opposite of Heimdall, who was friendly to mankind. Heimdall represented signalling beacons of fire and similarly controlled types of flames. Loki was the originator of many serious incidents within Asgard, and he also fathered the vile Fenris Wolf, the beast that eventually devoured Odin at the world's end, during Ragnarok.

The Vanir

This group of gods included Njord and his twin children, Frey and Freya. An older set of gods than the Aesir, these were predominantly agricultural beings, representing fertility, crop harvests and the Earth as a whole, along with wisdom, nature, magic and the ability to see into the future. Their abode was in Vanaheim, or the Home of the Vanir.

The world tree, Yggdrasil, was said to have the Nine Worlds amongst its roots and branches. Odin's eight-legged steed, Sleipnir, carried him freely between the nine worlds.

5: THE NINE WORLDS

Midgard   World of Humans

Midgard *(middle earth)* is located in the middle of three levels, below Asgard and Vanaheim. It's connected to Asgard by the Rainbow Bridge, Bifrost, and is surrounded by a huge, impassable ocean. In the ocean dwells a huge sea serpent, the Midgard Serpent. The serpent is so vast that it encircles the whole world, and bites its own tail. Odin and his two brothers, Vili and Ve, created the first humans, carving men from an ash log, and women from an elm log.

Niflheim   World of the Serpent Nidhog

Niflheim *(Mist Home)* is the darkest and coldest world. It was the first of the nine worlds, and is situated in the northern region of Ginnungagap (the original void). Niflheim is home to the eldest of the three wells, called Hvergelmir, which is a bubbling, boiling spring protected by the huge serpent called Nidhog.

Jotunheim   World of the Giants

Jotunheim is the home of the Jotuns (giants). They are the sworn enemies of the Aesir, and these two races are in constant conflict. Jotunheim consists mostly of rocks, wilderness and dense forests, so the giants live by catching fish in the rivers, and hunting animals in the forest; there is no fertile land in Jotunheim. This world was created from the body of the first Jotun, Ymir, after Odin and his brothers, Vili and Ve, killed him.

Although the Jotuns and the Aesir are constantly fighting, it also happens from time to time that love affairs crop up. Odin, Thor and a few others had lovers who were Jotuns. Loki also came from Jotunheim, but he was accepted by the Aesir and lived in Asgard. Jotunheim is separated from Asgard by the river Iving, which never freezes over. Mimir's Well of Wisdom is in Jotunheim, beneath the Midgard root of the ash tree Yggdrasil.

Muspelheim   World of Fire

Muspelheim was created far to the south of the nine worlds. It's a burning hot place, filled with lava, flames, sparks and soot, and it's the home of the fire giants and fire demons, all of whom are ruled by the giant Surt. He is a sworn enemy of the Aesir. Surt will ride out with his flaming sword in his hand at Ragnarok, the end of the worlds, and he will then attack Asgard (which is the home of the gods), turning it into a flaming inferno.

Vanaheim   Home of the Vanir Gods

Vanaheim is the home of the Vanir gods, an old branch of the Norse deities. The Vanir are masters of sorcery and magic. They are also widely acknowledged for their talent in predicting the future. Nobody knows where exactly Vanaheim is located, or even what it really looks like. When the war between the Aesir and the Vanir ended, three of the Vanir came to live in Asgard, these being Njord and his children Freya and Frey.

Alfheim   World of the Fair Elves

Alfheim is near Asgard in the worldly system. The fair elves are beautiful creatures, and they are considered guardian angels. The fair elves are minor gods of nature and fertility; they can help or hinder humans by using their knowledge of magic. They also often inspire works of art or music. The god Freyr rules Alfheim.

Swartalfheim World of the Dark Elves

Swartalfheim is the home of the dark elves. The dark elves can't stand the sun, so they live underground. They are hideous and are nothing but trouble to the human race. A polite description would be "extremely annoying". However, the gods used them to create Gleipnir, the impossibly strong binding that held captive the Fenris Wolf until Ragnarok. While the monstrous wolf was being bound, it managed to bite off Tyr's right hand.

Helheim   *World of the Dishonoured Dead*

By "dishonoured dead", the ancients meant those who didn't die in battle. Death in battle was the only way to avoid Helheim, a rather unpleasant place in which to end up. Ruled by Hel, this world was the final destination for many unfortunate souls, including Odin's son, Baldur. Baldur was everyone's favourite, except for the spiteful Loki, who carefully planned his "accidental" death. All Odin's efforts to retrieve Baldur were fruitless.

Asgard   *Home of the Aesir Gods*

High up, above the other worlds, is Asgard, the home of the Aesir gods and goddesses. The male gods in Asgard are called Aesir, and the female gods are called Asynjur. Odin rules Asgard, and is the head of the Aesir. He is married to Frigga, the Queen of the Aesir. Inside the gates of Asgard is Valhalla, the place where Vikings who died in battle reside in the afterlife.

Half the dead Vikings would come to Valhalla; the other half are given to the goddess Freya. She always has the first choice from the dead warriors. Every morning, the Vikings in Valhalla would take up their weapons and armour, then walk out to the plains in Asgard and fight, because it was immaterial whether they were wounded or dismembered; when the great dinner in the evening came, they were all restored to normal so they could enjoy the night's revels.

6: SYMBOLS OF THE RUNES

The Symbols of the Runes

FREYA'S AETT		TYR'S AETT	
Fehu	ᚠ	Tiwaz	ᛏ
Uruz	ᚢ	Berkano	ᛒ
Thurisaz	ᚦ	Ehwaz	ᛖ
Ansuz	ᚨ	Mannaz	ᛗ
Raido	ᚱ	Laguz	ᛚ
Kaunaz	ᚲ	Inguz	ᛜ
Gebo	ᚷ	Othila	ᛟ
Wunjo	ᚹ	Dagaz	ᛞ

HAGAL'S AETT	
Hagalaz	ᚺ
Nauthiz	ᚾ
Isa	ᛁ
Jera	ᛃ
Eihwaz	ᛇ
Pertho	ᛈ
Algiz	ᛉ
Sowelo	ᛊ

7: Making or Buying your Runes

If you like making your own tools and artefacts, you can make your own set of Runes, but a shop-bought set will work perfectly well, too.

The traditional way of making Runes is to cut a thin branch from a nut or fruit-bearing tree, remembering to thank the tree, and leaving a silver coin at its base in payment.

Slice the branch into 25 coin-shaped pieces, and then carve or paint the Rune symbols onto the pieces. A coat of clear varnish will finish the job.

Another method is to cut square shapes out of a flat piece of wood, and then paint and varnish them as mentioned above.

You can also make Rune cards, which would be shuffled instead of shaken in a bag, and while the latter is the more traditional method, whatever you do, the Runes will work just fine.

If you buy a set from a shop or online, you will need to cleanse the pieces before starting to work with them. This is because they will have picked up vibes from the people who made them, or those who handled them while they were in the shop or on the stand at a psychic fair before you bought them.

Cleansing and Preparing your Runes
If the Runes are stone or crystal, wash them in bottled spring water (even wooden Runes may be able to stand a quick dunk.)

Lay all the Runes out on a clean cloth and then imagine a bright, white light beaming down on them from the universe, allowing the light to wash around the Runes.

If you like, you can then hold each Rune in the smoke of an incense stick for a few moments.

Finally, bless your Runes, ask them to give help to all who need it, and put them away until you need to use them.

While we're on the subject of spiritual tools, it's traditional to keep Runes in a special bag. However, I'm a great believer in people doing what feels right for them, so choose a box, bag or tin that you like for your Runes. Keep all such tools away from children and pets, preferably above head-height and therefore, closer to heaven.

8: FREYA'S AETT

The ancient Germanic tribes called the runic alphabet the "Futhark", after the sound of the first letters of the first six Runes: Fehu, Uruz Thurisaz, Ansuz, Raido and Kaunaz.

Freya's Aett represents the beginning of all things and the primordial forces of fire and ice, from which the first creatures emerged. All the Runes in this Aett have a fresh feeling about them, and a sense that all things are possible.

CONNECTIONS	
Fehu	The cow, Audhumla
Uruz	The wild bull
Thurisaz	The giant, Ymir
Ansuz	A god
Raido	The kick-start that set life into motion
Kaunaz	A bonfire, representing the division of day and night
Gebo	The gods, led by Odin, giving the sacred trees the gift of life
Wunjo	Perfection and readiness for human life to begin

FEHU

Other Names:
FEOH and FE

Pronounced
F

In Brief

Fehu relates to the first living entity, the cow Audhumla. It emerged from the primordial fire and ice at the dawn of history. As nothing else existed at that time, the cow licked at a block of ice, which action released Ymir, the giant from whom sprang all the other giants, the gods and humans. It is unclear whether Ymir was released from the ice, or whether she was fashioned from the block of by the cow's licking tongue. In any event, she tended and cared for all her "offspring" like any other mother figure.

Fehu is also linked to some of the Vanir gods, including Njord and his children, Frey and Freya. The latter two are also associated with fertility and wealth.

Key Attributes

The connection with Audhumla, the cow, is a clear association with wealth and financial matters. Cattle were an important measure of a person's standing, being valuable for ploughing the fields, pulling a cart and providing milk and meat for the table. A responsible nature in managing one's wealth is needed, and Fehu helps in achieving this goal. When this Rune is seen in a reading, you can expect good fortune in the foreseeable future. Other possessions are also included in the meaning and should be managed well to avoid shortages in hard times. Ancient peoples were always careful to keep foodstuffs by in the winter or in times of war. Whether rich or poor, Fehu is a fortunate sign in a reading.

Reversed Meaning

Take care, as this indicates a material loss of some kind, possibly from making a poor investment decision, being robbed of your possessions or any other reversal in your fortunes. The loss of a good friend or loved one may be indicated, but chances are that this will be a temporary issue, because even when reversed, Fehu is a kindly and helpful Rune. A problem with fertility may arise.

URUZ

Other Names:
Also called UR

Pronounced:
U or OO

In Brief
Uruz formed a pair with Audhumla, the first world being. Uruz has a masculine nature and is associated with the ancient wild bulls of the northern territories, the massive Auroch. These were untamed, aggressive animals, far larger than today's bulls and bison, and Uruz links with the very macho god, Thor. He was the thunder god, the sworn enemy of the giants, and much respected by the other gods. Thor's hammer, forged for him by the underground elves, is a legendary weapon.

Key Attributes
Related to the eldest Norn, Urd, this Rune also has a close association with the Vanir gods. A primal meaning includes rebelling against restraint, protection of one's own family and possessions – principally land and larger assets.

In a reading, Uruz indicates the likelihood of improvement in your working environment or career trends, albeit that these have to be earned. Energy, courage and strength will pool your resources, but there is always the warning not to use these powerful tools to excess; you have to be responsible and not take on more than you can reasonably cope with.

In other areas, sound health or speedy recovery from illness is indicated. Many positive and manly links are shown, including initiative, stamina, fertility and the ability to use your intelligence in harnessing the benefits endowed by this Rune.

Reversed Meaning

Typically, the opposite of the positive aspects are indicated, with the need to take care when tempted to make rash decisions. Lack of energy, mental and physical weakness are evident. In the really negative possibilities, you may find unreasonable harshness, brutal abuse towards others, and the likelihood of such oppressive treatment being levelled at you. Events may seem overwhelming, so it is best to ride out the storm while keeping a low profile.

However, in most cases, these extremes aren't apparent, and the Rune may simply be indicating a lack of vitality and low self-esteem, so it's appropriate not to expect the worst.

THURISAZ

Other Names:
Thurisa, Thorn, Thauris, Thurs

Pronounced:
TH

In Brief
Associated with the god Thor, part of the Rune's name is still seen in the English words Thursday and Thorn. Thor was a god amongst gods, a powerful being with whom no one wished to argue or fight, especially with Thor's hammer looming in the vicinity. This weapon would return by itself when thrown, so it was handy to use at a distance as well as in close combat. This Rune's origins also connect with the Thursur giants, and have the dual nature of combative destruction and protective strength. Either face is presented depending upon the circumstances.

Key Attributes
You have to know your own strengths and weaknesses when this Rune is present, because you may experience transformation and chaotic behaviour, forcing you to think swiftly before acting. Its powerful nature is such that it can change the meanings of other Runes near it in a reading. In a way, it can approximate the attributes of Pluto in an astrological sense, as the destruction and tearing apart of structures is often followed by reconstruction that is later seen to have been a necessary act of renewal.

Reversed Meaning
You may walk into a trap set by an enemy, so avoid acting without thinking or being greedy. The latter is always unwise in any event, and with this Rune, the saying: "there's no such thing as a free lunch" is perfectly apt. Your luck may be running out, or you may be behaving obstinately to the extent that you experience reprisals, and in either case, it's best not to make any major decisions for a while.

ANSUZ

Other Names:
Oss, Ansur

Pronounced:
Either A or O

In Brief
Linked to the mouth, speech, breath and inspiration. Also called the "god Rune", due to its association with the gods, principally Odin, who brought the knowledge of all the Runes back to Asgard and humanity.

Key Attributes
Odin's two ravens, Hugin and Munin, are also linked to this Rune, and communication is thus represented by the birds, which acted as messengers. Odin's self-inflicted sacrifice was in the branches of the world tree, Yggdrasil. This being an ash tree, Ansuz has that link, too. Learning and wisdom are Ansuz' intellectual attributes, with the added ability to get out of tricky situations by using one's wits. The Rune may also indicate the approach of an energetic and more intellectually gifted companion who will assist with an exit strategy in the event of difficulties. Ansuz is a Rune of consciousness and awareness.

Reversed Meaning
This can mean a difficulty in communicating your thoughts, as is the case in astrology when the planet Mercury turns retrograde. There may be a physical affliction, such as a sore throat, as well as a mental blockage. Travel and messages of any kind may be negatively affected. In a further inversion, you may be subjected to lies, deceit, theft and false or incorrect advice.

RAIDO

Other Names:
Rad, Reid, Raid

Pronounced:
R

In Brief

The sun is the main heavenly connection here, and journeys, whether for business or pleasure, will go well. Honourable behaviour and being able to tell right from wrong. The Rune is linked to Mugwort, which was said to be a healing herb, so this Rune links to health matters.

Key Attributes

Transportation - mainly by land – including carts, horses and nowadays, rail or motor vehicles. Leadership, moral responsibility, integrity and respect for fellow men, and spiritual journeys are all indicated here. The Rune teaches you to use your abilities wisely and efficiently, thus achieving your goals swiftly, surely and successfully, albeit that sometimes difficulties intervene. Official and legal matters will resolve in your favour, but not by chance, because your own abilities will bring the desired solutions.

Reversed Meaning

You may find various disruptions in your plans and projects, with delays being a feature. This doesn't mean you should give up, it means you will have to fight more persistently and forcefully to get what you want. A solution to one issue may turn out to be a fresh hindrance in another direction. Keep an eye on the overall scenario, don't get bogged down by small problems, and remember that nothing lasts forever – you can still succeed!

KAUNAZ

Other Names:
Cen, Ken, Kaun

Pronounced:
K or hard C

In Brief

Enlightenment through the purification of a flaming torch, artistry, intellectual and physical creativity; all these are part of Kaunaz's list of attributes. Its light keeps the darkness of night at bay and helps protect the traveller, while the student can read under its bright rays. Mental illumination and higher levels of knowledge are involved here. On the other hand, the heat of a torch can also hurt, so another connection of this Rune is with ulcers, which can feel aflame if untreated.

Key Attributes

Kaunaz is the Rune of Heimdall, a son of Odin's who was the guardian or gatekeeper of the gods in Asgard. He kept humans and giants from crossing Bifrost, the Rainbow Bridge, into Asgard. This task was faithfully maintained until the time of Ragnarok, when everything fell apart in the final conflict between gods and all other beings in the Norse universe. Heimdall's trusty creature was the owl, another sign of learning and of passing on knowledge to others. Bonfires and beacon signals between mountains were also the province of Heimdall.

Interesting to know is the fact that Kaunaz includes passion, physical love and loving relationships. It can mean a new love, or a new path of discovery, always with a feeling of safety, as if the gods were looking kindly on your affairs.

Reversed Meaning

The positive aspects of Kaunaz can turn to loss of prospects, friendships or love relationships, and you may feel adrift and without purpose in life. These feelings will only be temporary, but they are nevertheless depressing at the time. Perhaps the past has been holding on to your thoughts too much, and it may be time to move on with a fresh view of life or work. The right steps to take will become apparent, you will learn the life lessons required, and the light of Kaunaz will re-enter your life.

GEBO

Other Names:
Gyfu

Pronounced:
G

In Brief

The ancients partnered Gebo with cattle, their main form of wealth. However, the key here is to be conscious of the risk of over-generous behaviour, which can be as bad as miserliness. Tethered to two gods in particular – Odin and Thor – Gebo's influence is seen in both; Odin, as the titular head of the Aesir pantheon, was in an ideal position to bestow gifts onto others. For example, he wore a precious arm ring called Draupnir, which replicated itself eightfold every nine days. These new rings would be given away at Odin's pleasure. One of Thor's duties was to preserve order and regulate events in the Norse universe, which slots in well with Gebo.

Key Attributes

The giving of gifts, as well as receiving favours, have always been positive features of civilised societies. Whether as a mark of respect, an indication of affection, or a symbolic and political gesture, Gebo is involved. Balance is necessary - generosity in one direction while ignoring others is a mark of imbalance, incurring resentment and even hostility.

Helping someone out is another attribute of Gebo's, and the issue of not overdoing things is another warning to maintain balance. It's not good to allow others to become dependent on your favours, so think before acting. Time and energy are as much a commodity as many other things, so don't allow others to drain you of these, either.

Reversed Meaning

Gebo is the first Rune out of all twenty-four that has no reversed meaning. This is clear from its icon, which looks the same, whether reversed or not.

WUNJO

Other Names:
Wynn, wynnju, vend

Pronounced:
W or V

In Brief

This is a Rune of happiness, domestic contentment, love and good fortune. It is also connected to physical beauty, wind, open spaces and clouds in a sunny sky. A really positive and harmonious Rune, which, unsurprisingly, is the Rune of Frigga, the epitome of all that is desirable in a wife. Frigga of course, was the wife of Odin, and none could match their bond and happiness with each other. Not that that stopped Odin from the occasional lusty indiscretion or five, but there were no doubt different standards to ours in those days, and there was never a hint of Odin being thus distracted for any length of time.

Key Attributes

Other attributes of Wunjo are weddings, happy endings, comfort and attraction that may blossom into a strong relationship. Matchmaking is indicated, and there seems to be no end to the favourable aspects inherent in this Rune. Unconditional love, good news and good fortune in creating a happy home are all indicated by Wunjo.

The appearance of this Rune in a reading may mean, for an unattached person, the likelihood of an attractive partner turning up out of the blue. The Vikings prized fair complexions and hair, so these attributes may be on the cards, but such features aren't necessarily the order of the day in our times, and other possibilities are also possible. Developing affairs may be of a business nature, but personal, romantic relationships are more likely.

Reversed Meaning

When inverted, the reading may warn that prospective partners aren't quite what they seem to be – what's on the surface isn't necessarily what's inside, so take care before getting too involved too soon. Major decisions should be delayed if possible, and closely investigated. Traditionally, it was recommended that personal decisions be postponed for three months, and business matters postponed for three days when Wunjo is reversed.

9: HAGAL'S AETT

In Hagal's Aett, the Runes begin to define some of the less joyful areas of life, and more of the destructive forces one is bound to come across sooner or later. However, once these challenges have been dealt with, there is time for joyful celebration. The seasons covered are winter and spring. Five of Hagal's Runes have no inverted interpretations. Not much is known about Hagal, and there is speculation the he is also known as Heimdall.

CONNECTIONS	
Hagalaz	Urd, Hel, hail, rain
Nauthiz	Verdandi, Norn of the future, necessity
Isa	Skuld, Norn of the present, ice, cold, iron
Jera	Baldur, joy, merriment, celebration
Eihwaz	Ullr, flexibility
Pertho	Frigga, the three Norns, possibilities, fate
Algiz	Heimdall, Valkyries, healing, safety
Sowelo	Thor, Baldur, inner self, love, poetic justice

HAGALAZ

Other Names:
Hagal

Pronounced:
H

In Brief

Grim connections here; Hel, the goddess who ruled Helheim, world of the dishonoured dead, Urd, Norn of the past, and Hagal's link to the destructive forces of hail and rain. Heimdall, guardian of the Rainbow Bridge – until Ragnarok looms - is a more beneficial influence. One's thoughts inevitably ponder the finite nature of life, because Ragnarok is the Norse equivalent of Armageddon.

Key Attributes

Hagalaz is the force that controls events in life, reminding us that we are not in full control of the world, let alone of ourselves. It is concerned with any mysterious, alarming and sudden challenges or problems, including divorce, death in the family, illness or a financial downturn. It may simply refer to far less traumatic events, such as a delayed vacation or journey, or perhaps a small leak in the roof.

It is essential to realise that nothing lasts forever – even unpleasant things. So, you have to be patient, ride out the storm, and there will be light at the end of the metaphorical tunnel. Renewal invariably means improvement, and the future is very likely to be much better.

Reversed Meaning

This Rune has no inverted meaning, so one can only note that some effects may be more difficult than expected. You may lose control of your environment, you may experience puzzling limitations in otherwise normal abilities, and you should certainly be extremely cautious in making plans or taking major decisions until the effects of Hagalaz have dissipated.

NAUTHIZ

Other Names:
Nyd, Naud

Pronounced:
N

In Brief
A driving force indeed, Nauthiz is the epitome of needs or necessity, whether physical and sexual, ambition in your career, or any form of desire to improve your lot in life. In moderation and under control, this is a positive Rune, but beware the consequences of becoming greedy, when the phrase "letting loose the hounds of hell", might take on a whole new meaning.

Key Attributes
The prime meaning here can be the drive for survival. This is an imperative for all living things, without which, extinct species would abound. The intention is clear – don't ever give up. At work, at home, or in dire circumstances, you must persevere. If you don't try and try again, you have little chance of succeeding in life. Remember that this Rune may place restrictions on you, but it also gives you the strength to plough through life's challenges. You may feel hard done by, but there is always someone who is worse off than you are, and there is no celestial mandate that says that you should have everything you want. If you have what you need, that is terrific and you should thank your lucky stars.

Nauthiz is connected to Niflheim, home of the huge serpent, Nidhog. Negative thoughts and feelings from this direction may seem overpowering, but they are all in the mind, and with this Rune, the only thing that can defeat you is you yourself.

Reversed Meaning

The stresses of the upright Rune are exaggerated when inverted. Time to be even more determined than ever to survive and prosper, at work, at home, with your loved ones and the environment as a whole. Avoid grasping at straws, avoid desperate behaviour, as that is a sure-fire attraction for scammers and other villains who can practically smell when someone is in difficulty. There is no free lunch, pyramid schemes and other get-rich-quick investment offers can be disastrous. Keep your head, make no hasty decisions, and if in any doubt, talk to someone who you know to be a wise and unbiased mentor. In fact, nowadays, the Internet can be such a valuable resource that it's hard to remember how we coped before the likes of Google, because there, you can find help and guidance in seconds for practically any question you can think of.

ISA

Other Names:
Is, Iss

Pronounced:
EE as in "eat"

In Brief

The idea relates to coldness, ice and hard, unyielding matter such as iron. Also bitter reality. Development of concentration and self-control are the means of working together with this Rune. It would be best to work with it, as it's unlikely that you can overpower its exacting demands. Change and adaptation aren't in vogue with Isa in the picture; preferably continue just as you have done all along, and don't make waves – at work or at home. Give yourself time to strengthen your spiritual self. All the above is confirmed by the Rune's association with Verdandi, goddess Norn of the present. Her aloof nature, iron will and determination are irresistible.

Key Attributes

Patience. Nothing is going to move quickly, whatever cloud is hanging over you. In business, you will likely experience delay after delay, and at home, a cold, unemotional wind may drift across relationships. Is there any silver lining to this dreary cloud? Well, you may find that those pesky delays have given you time to reconsider your plans, think things over thoroughly, and come up with a better answer to whatever you intended doing. Don't forget, Isa has only temporary sway over your life – it passes fairly soon, and you can then move on, hopefully with a better and more confident attitude than before.

Reversed Meaning

There is no reversed meaning for Isa.

JERA

Other Names:
Ar, Jer

Pronounced:
J or Y

In Brief

The word means "year", and connections are with the harvest, favourable events and the celebrations after a good harvest. The winter solstice is also within Jera's remit; although it's a rather cold time of year, everything starts to warm up as the sun starts to grow stronger from this time forward. Similarly, Jera is the twelfth Rune, marking the midpoint in the Elder Futhark. Completion of cycles and forthcoming expectations are marked by this Rune, along with the pleasure of having worked hard and thus earned / reaped the rewards accordingly.

Key Attributes

The link to harvesting extends to help in the garden and growing crops. In a reading, Jera can indicate that you would be well placed to achieve satisfaction with any project involving the land, or indeed, many creative endeavours intended to bring ideas into physical manifestation. There is a peaceful air about Jera, so you should experience a steady, uninterrupted flow through to conclusion of the tasks in hand. This Rune is attuned to the harmonies of life, it doesn't bring about swift changes, it helps to progress matters peacefully and gradually. Somehow, under the influence of Jera, timing of events takes on the semblance of an impeccably performed dance routine, seemingly with little effort. As long as you do your part positively, Jera will match and guide you through the most difficult responsibilities. Legal matters and contracts, especially in connection with land or a new home, flow more easily under this Rune's influence.

Reversed Meaning

Jera has no reversed meaning, but in the event of a negative impact, you may expect just a mild reduction in matters affected by this Rune.

EIHWAZ

Other Names:
Eoh, Ihwaz

Pronounced:
EI as in "rise"

In Brief
The Norse spiritual connection here is to trees, and in particular, the yew tree. The mysteries of life and death, initiation rites, communication with those who have passed on and the search for enlightenment are the main attributes of Eihwaz. Wisdom and rebirth feature as well.

Key Attributes
In a reading, Eihwaz assures you of protection in your search for self-enlightenment and other matters to do with the spirit world. It insists that you walk the path of righteousness, and avoid temptations. Progress on a spiritual path calls for dedication, patience and compassion. Such lessons become easier when Eihwaz is involved, so you should confront any impediments with determination, and you will find that they aren't anywhere near as hard as at first sight. Magical practice is aided by this Rune, so your spells will be more effective than usual. On a more physical level, Eihwaz connects with hunting, and the best bows were made from yew trees. Synthetic materials are often used nowadays, but there is a unique satisfaction when using natural wood to make the bow. Strength and stability are also characteristics of this Rune.

Reversed Meaning
This is another example of a Rune having no reversed meaning.

PERTHO

Other Names:
Perth, Peorth, Peoro

Pronounced:
P

In Brief
Associated with beginnings, the cycle of birth and death, mysteries and things hidden from view. Supernatural events and abilities are evident. Pertho can precipitate unanticipated changes, often as positive improvements in the status quo. Your subconscious mind contains an amazing amount of knowledge, and Pertho helps you to access the information needed to understand deep spiritual improvement.

Key Attributes
Pertho also links with lighter matters, such as games and amusements, including competitive sports and gambling, where chance plays a major role. However, it is mainly concerned with more serious matters and things to be revealed that are beyond our control. Prophetic dreams and visions belong to Pertho. If Pertho is the first Rune out of the Rune bag, then go no further with the reading; the outcome is sealed, not to be known at this point in time. Leave things for another day. If Pertho appears later in the reading, then you will find answers much more readily, and you can count on fate taking a favourable part in your near future.

Reversed Meaning
A radical change from the upright meanings, with fate taking matters out of your hands and shaping them in a destructive manner. You may feel penalised for some reason, but you need not have done anything harmful - Pertho is a law unto itself. Just take care, avoid gambling at all costs, start nothing new. Hidden secrets may emerge, your past may arise to humble you and put paid to all your plans.

ALGIZ

Other Names:
Eolh, Algz, Elhaz

Pronounced:
Z

In Brief
Algiz relates to the white elk and reeds, sedge and other water loving plants. The lime tree is also connected. The legendary Valkyries, at least some of whom were daughters of Odin's wife, Frigga, adopted this Rune, endowing it with the ability of communicating with humans and gods alike. The Valkyries would scour battlefields for dead warriors worthy of admission to Valhalla. Veritable shape-shifters, they often took the form of birds such as crows, and some sources believe that the shape of this Rune emulates a bird's footprint. Indicated are protection from enemies, defence of loved ones, and connections to animals of all kinds.

Key Attributes
The god Heimdall is also associated with Algiz, because the light given by this Rune is a necessary tool in his role as guardian of the Rainbow Bridge. A powerful Rune of protection, Algiz confirms the positive results of your endeavours and encourages you to trust your feelings and instincts.

As the top rated Rune for healing and protection, Algiz tells you that you are shielded from harm and that a health problem will be overcome. The main inference is that you should value yourself, and cherish and implement your dreams and aspirations, albeit within reason. Take no notice of pressure and the demands of others if these would hold you back from your own principles and wishes. Not a selfish Rune, Algiz just ensures that you care for yourself properly. If you don't look after yourself properly, then how would you be able to give any attention to others?

Reversed Meaning

Here, the meaning is to amplify the upright situation; you need to give far more attention to yourself and your own needs than you thought was adequate. Health problems may be evident, or will appear in the near future, and extra care will be needed. Other people may not be aware of your needs, or may even refuse to accept that you are just human. When Algiz is inverted, insensitivity from others is a persistent feature, and you may have to take drastic action to get away from such a destructive environment. Either get rid of such people, or remove yourself from their presence, no matter what they say or think. You may be in a weak physical and mental state, so it's probably best just to get away from everybody so you can recover in peace. Take a break.

SOWELO

Other Names:
Sol, Sigil, Sowelu

Pronounced:
S

In Brief
This is the sun Rune. It expresses clear vision, light, fertility and luck. Growth and the natural life force that is a major survival attribute in all living beings. The sun enables crops to grow, living things to flourish and prosper. Connections are the enduring oak tree, the eagle and mistletoe. The shape of this Rune reminds you of a thunderbolt, and yes, it is linked to the almighty Thor, god of thunder.

Key Attributes
Hard to list all that this Rune touches upon, it has so wide a remit; it symbolises success, enlightenment, joy, the law, the promise of enduring goodness and the revelation of truth in all its forms. What part of life is not dependent upon the sun? Truly a top Rune to find in a reading! Happiness and well-being reign when Sowelo is present, justice and providence feature prominently. In sporting events, you are singled out for peak performance, whether winning or not. The implications are the same, whether in matters of love, work, the home, travel and so on and on.

Reversed Meaning
How could there be a negative side to this Rune? There is no reversed meaning, and the only less-than-ideal issue would be an excess of zeal, overconfident behaviour, or absolute burnout from going too far in whatever you may be doing. This is the time to apply the ancient Greek saying: *"pan metron ariston"*, or "moderation in all things."

10: TYR'S AETT

Tyr's Aett refers to the kind of situations that we all deal with on a daily basis, along with the wider concerns of society in general. It also brings things to a conclusion. This Aett relates to the world around us, as well as to ourselves.

CONNECTIONS	
Tiwaz	Tyr, firm contracts, agreements
Berkano	Frigga, the Mother Goddess, birth, living things
Ehwaz	Frey, Ing, Sleipnir, animals, quests
Mannaz	Heimdall, Rigr, mankind
Laguz	Njord, divine love
Inguz	Ing, Frey, well-being, fertility
Othila	Odin, rulership, loyalty, royalty
Dagaz	Heimdall, Loki, beginnings and endings

TIWAZ

Other Names:
Tyr, Teiwaz, Tiw

Pronounced:
T

In Brief

This is the Rune of the war god, Tyr. Besides being the role model and protector for valiant warriors, he stood for fairness, justice and binding agreements. Also linked to the pole star, which is used by sailors for navigation, Tiwaz thus promises guidance and reliable knowledge to assist those who travel long distances. Tyr lost his right hand to the Fenris Wolf's bite when the gods were trying to bind the destructive monster wolf. His Rune signifies that at times, one may have to sacrifice something precious to achieve a greater goal.

Key Attributes

Marriage vows are an enduring example of the binding agreements typically sanctioned by Tiwaz. There is nevertheless a strong masculine air about the Rune, so contracts and other legal associations have a leaning in favour of a male participant. In marriage, the wife might need to put her own needs last for a while, to care for children and to ensure that the relationship remains steady.

Successful sporting achievements are the order of the day under this Rune's influence, and in business matters as well. Being firmly convinced in your beliefs ensures that you won't falter in the middle of any competitive endeavours. Courage, clear vision and selfless ideals come into play when Tiwaz is present. A partnership in business could fail if both or all parties involved have strong personalities, because the great Tyr bows to no one, so you need to be the acknowledged boss of the enterprise. Fortunately, you are likely to make all the right decisions, making it easier for others to listen to you.

Reversed Meaning

When reversed, the honourable qualities mentioned above are inverted. Shallow relationships, selfishness, cowardly behaviour and lack of faith in oneself are typical. In a love relationship, the woman would do well to think twice before committing herself. Alternatively, the relationship may be, to put it mildly, less than enduring. Injustice and greed may be evident.

BERKANO

Other Names:
Bjarkan, Beork, Berkana

Pronounced:
B

In Brief
A feminine nature is relevant to this Rune, so motherhood and domestic matters are to the fore. The birch tree is the plant association here, as is the swan for its bird symbol, and agriculture in general is highlighted. Healers, herbal experts and women are part of the picture. With femininity involved, so is Frigga, the epitome of the female sex in the Vikings' godly pantheon.

Key Attributes
Key to Berkano are the images of familial protection, nurture and birth. All the feminine traits are embodied here, although a sensitive, supportive male may appear in a reading. Fertility and motherhood are important considerations, but also linked are new ideas, imaginative thinking and the romance of a new love affair. A happy family home, contentment and a peaceful environment are all shown here.

Reversed Meaning
Family worries, whether in health, financial or accidental are most common with an inverted Berkano. Infertility is another possibility. Events or celebrations may be forestalled or cancelled. In any event, you would find that stagnation reigns, so plans and projects are unlikely to come to fruition. Whatever the position, you should closely examine and evaluate your own views and attitudes within the family group, because the root cause of the problems may in your nature and beliefs. So, things may need to change or be adapted to current circumstances.

EHWAZ

Other Names:
Eoh, Eih, Eow

Pronounced:
E as in "then"

In Brief
Although the names are similar, Ehwaz has no relation to the Rune "Eihwaz" in Hagal's Aett. Ehwaz means "horse", and is linked to Odin's trusty, eight-legged steed, Sleipnir, which carried Odin on journeys between all the nine worlds.

Key Attributes
Having a travel relationship in worlds beyond ours means that Ehwaz is concerned with spiritual travel, whether psychically or in astral travel. Protection is part of the Rune's function, so you can rest assured you won't get into spiritual difficulties while away from your body. There is a later addition to the meaning of this Rune, with an Anglo-Saxon bond to Hengist and Horsa; they were Germanic brothers who established a kingdom in the Kent area of England in the fifth century AD. Their names mean, respectively, "stallion" and "horse". To a lesser degree, domesticated animals other than horses are connected to Ehwaz, as are the apple tree, the ash tree and the herb ragwort.

In the modern world, one inference is the facilitation of developments in transport, communication and especially the Internet, which, let's face it, is considered an "off-worldly" means of verbal, visual and virtual communication that is absolutely essential.

Generally speaking, Ehwaz is a beneficial Rune, showing changes for the better – often rapidly, befitting its fleet-footed equine relationship. It is also considered to improve or increase the effects of other Runes in the reading.

Reversed Meaning

People may be out of sync with you and your plans, setbacks may happen involving travel or communications. Trying to get others to fit in with you will only get their backs up and make things worse. Very likely, you should put business and travel plans on hold for a while. Be alert to the possibility of ill health in your pets and other domestic animals, and take pro-active steps where possible; for one thing, ensure that your pets' vaccinations are up to date.

MANNAZ

Other Names:
Madr, Mann, Manna, Mannuz

Pronounced:
M

In Brief

The connection is to mankind, male and female. Human beings are sentient, capable of proactive behaviour and foresight, which traits are invaluable on group levels. The Rune takes on the bigger picture rather than just an individual one, and its bond with protection and assistance is principally on the scale of society as a whole, along with smaller groups.

Key Attributes

Mannaz shows just how hard life was in ancient times, so invoking help in whatever fashion possible was key to a long life. Today's problems are different but just as crucial, so Mannaz is as valuable as ever in a reading, as it helps to maintain a stable level of social system and order. Your part and support of the infrastructure is essential, as is that of every one else. With the help of Mannaz, you will be quite clear about your standing and value within the community.

In a societal structure, it is always a good idea to reflect on your personal ideals and beliefs, to check whether you might be straying from the positive changes that happen from time to time. Additionally, you may be able to influence for the better matters that fall within your skill set or professional training. Remember that nothing ever stands still – either it grows and improves, or it falls behind and wastes away. Mind you, it's also good to avoid simply being critical of systems or others from a personal viewpoint, so always make sure you have all the facts and data in front of you before speaking out. Mannaz is not a Rune of speed and haste, so be thorough in your actions.

Reversed Meaning

Sadly, this may mean that you have an enemy who is actively hostile to you. Not necessarily in a physical manner, but clearly wanting to damage you, your position in a group or at work, or even at home in one way or another. Check the next Rune in the reading for further enlightenment.

The alternative inference may be that you have an intractable problem and you see no way out of it. You may be overstating the scope of the problem, so it's vital that you seek outside, valued guidance before retreating or making an unsatisfactory decision. Be really open in assessing the matter, as it could have arisen from your own shortcomings, which are never easy to acknowledge.

LAGUZ

Other Names:
Logi, Lagu, Lagaz

Pronounced:
L

In Brief
Ideally described in the "Icelandic Rune Poem", Laguz is closely connected to water, both fresh and salt, as in the oceans. The vertical shape of the Rune may indicate a swelling tide. Animal connections are to the otter and the seal, along with the seagull and cormorant, all of which are mainly seen around coastal waters. Here we find the kindly god Njord, a Vanir god and father of Frey and Freya. Njord overlooks the essential work of fishing and boats including sailing vessels. Other protected themes under Njord's control are lakes, rivers and streams, fjords, harbours and estuaries. Expect fair weather for sailing when this Rune comes up in a reading.

Key Attributes
With the help of Laguz, your journeys – especially ones over water – are safeguarded, while the same can be said about internal, spiritual meditation and soul-searching. Even if you are feeling downhearted and powerless in some situation or other, Laguz will help, but you need to have patience – you can't rush Laguz. Besides the sea, this Rune has an interest in matters of spiritual and physical love, and helps you to prevail over relationship problems and spiritual shortcomings.

Water has long been connected to hidden secrets, sensitivity and emotional upsets. The astrological sign of Cancer, the crab, is a water sign and embodies emotions, ups and downs in the manner of the tides, and Laguz has very similar traits. A positive feature is that of intuition, and you may find this appears in times of distress.

Good luck and successful business dealings are indicated. Naturally, international trade (i.e. overseas) is particularly favourably influenced.

Reversed Meaning

Inverted meanings include excessive sensitivity, excessive emotional ups and downs, and a failure to pay attention to your normally stable mind. It's always critical to remember how you felt and what actions you used when feeling stable and unemotional. Use the same behaviours now, as that has to be more useful than random and hasty reactions. Worst of all would be to turn to drink or drugs, neither of which can improve anything. A parallel is to a drowning man, whose panicky struggles only tire him out. Best to concentrate on staying afloat instead.

INGUZ

Other Names:
Ing

Pronounced:
NG as in "wing"

In Brief

Although Ing was known as the horse god, there was a more dedicated link, to the boar. Many records identify Ing as the doorway to the spiritual levels, however, in the ancient Germanic tongues, Ing or Ying tends to mean "boy" or "lad", or even "son of". The Rune has the useful attribute of male fertility. Another connection here was to the Vanir deity, Frey, who was the reason for the boar link, as Frey liked to ride on a golden boar named Gullinbursti. The boar's bristles symbolised fields of wheat, which is another link for this Rune. Ing and Frey may have been one and the same, but the records aren't clear on this point. Ing may have been a real person, and some archives claim that the name "England" derived from a Germanic King called Ing.

Key Attributes

A change of job – for the better - is likely when Ing turns up in a reading. It may also indicate a fresh start in some other fashion, or good health, new ideas, projects that become really useful, and it helps to endow the questioner with the vigour needed to complete the project. This includes solving problems by finding intellectual solutions, and it helps in completing previous work that has to be finalised before starting on the new matter. The Rune can just mean that a spring-clean is due, in the home or at work. There may not be any immediate need for this, but you can expect some new project to appear shortly that warrants a clean slate.

If people around you are leaning on you, making demands that take up your time and energy, then you may need to identify the "leeches" and part from them. Life is too short to be inundated by the unwarranted demands of others. Indeed, you may deserve a break or holiday to recover from an excessive period under the strain of keeping other people happy at your own expense.

Reversed Meaning

There is no specific inverted meaning, but you may well find other negative Runes next to Inguz in the reading, and then, Inguz could be alerting you to the possibility that you are too weak or lazy to raise the energy or interest in taking up useful opportunities. This can hold you back from promotion at work, or other forms of development. Seek help from your spirit guides to get out of the potential mess in which you have landed.

OTHILA

Other Names:
Epel, Ethel, Othil, Othala

Pronounced:
O as in mould or bottle

In Brief
Relates to the home, family, inheritance and valuable possessions. Also connections to royalty or other high levels of nobility. Family matters and finances are handled sensibly, as well as farming responsibilities, duties to others, and sometimes giving up personal freedoms for the good of all. The godly link is to Odin himself, who epitomised personal sacrifice for the good of all when he hung himself from a branch of Yggdrasil, the world tree. He spent nine days and nights there, in order to win the knowledge of all the Runes, which then spread to the Norse gods and to humanity as well, thanks to Heimdall's kindliness.

Key Attributes
The association is with land and therefore the valuable assets raised thereon. Crops and herds of cattle demonstrate wealth and prosperity, stable values that stand the test of time, and the security you can derive from these possessions. They are worth working for and defending against thieves and con men.

Loyalty is the other major attribute, and this is what maintains local and regional stability. You need to understand this fully, and you are reminded of such obligations by Othila. By the same token, this Rune affirms the independence you seek and the group liberties that derive from an ordered and capable legal system. Odin's standards and presence are a constant guide and encouragement to you and others in your family or group. Responsibilities within the immediate family, more distant relatives, local communities and regions all fall under this Rune.

Reversed Meaning

Clearly, disloyalty and the overthrow of established rules and regulations are the direct characteristics of an inverted Othila. Arguments about inheritances and other possessions of value are likely, while theft and skulduggery loom close at hand. It's also to be expected that accidents and complex problems with machines and tools will appear. Disruption at work or at home to the established order will abound. The answer is simple: keep a clear head, avoid tempting offers and smooth talking individuals, and hold back from making decisions for the time being. If something is unavoidable, try to keep your actions simple and safe.

DAGAZ

Other Names:
Daeg, Daguz

Pronounced:
D

In Brief

Dagaz simply means "day", and the Rune has close connections to the best of days, those in the warmth and sun of summer. To the Nordic tribes, what else could compare to the absence of cold, rain and snow, typically expected for much of the time in the northern lands? Jera represents midwinter, and Dagaz is directly opposite Jera if the twenty-four Runes are laid out in a circle. These two are both Runes of change. However, while Jera represents gentle change, Dagaz' ministrations are more immediate. Trees for Dagaz are the rowan and Norwegian spruce, and the godly connection is to Thor, the god of thunder and lightning; rather apt, as Thor's lightning bolts are as swift and dazzling as this Rune's nature.

Key Attributes

Dagaz is the last of the twenty-four Runes, and the pack ends on a happy and prosperous note, embodying laughter, joy and the promise of amazing new developments. Things will happen very soon, whether you are prepared for change or not. Dagaz can also mean the end of a period of aggravation and the exposure of previously secret information. Here we have a source of unabated hope and happiness, served to the rich and the poor regardless of status.

If you have a pet project or job of work waiting in the wings, you may carry on without delay, as the promise is that of a flawless outcome to your full satisfaction. When you find new people coming into your life, be assured that they are friendly, but you are protected against villains in any event. Being a Rune of benevolent change, Dagaz signifies the ending and beginning of old and new respectively in your life. Good health is also in abundance.

Dagaz heralds a period of high spirits and can mean a break from the serious side of life, giving you the opportunity to relax and enjoy yourself. Life is now what you'd wish it to be, so make the most of it, because unfortunately, nothing lasts forever. Your childlike happiness extends to children in your family or circle of friends, and indications are that they will share in the good fortune and joy inherent in this Rune.

Reversed Meaning

No reversed meaning is recorded for Dagaz. If the Rune falls on its face or if it's surrounded by negative Runes, it still bears no hardship – it would just imply the end of a phase, but this would still be followed by the bright, new start of another cycle in your life, perhaps slightly less swiftly than would otherwise have been the case.

Wyrd, the Blank Rune

There are no records, either in ancient Germanic or Anglo-Saxon mythology, of a blank  Rune. It has been added to the pack of twenty-four much later in history, and has no alphabetical significance. Instead, it may be regarded as an independent omen that fate has taken, or will take, a firm hand in your affairs, be it for good or ill. Wyrd is the web that the Norns weave, and some records infer that the Norns are daughters of Wyrd. Either way, this Rune can be considered the spiritual judge and jury of mankind, setting out penalties for transgressions that it winkles out.

There is, fortunately, a good and favourable side to Wyrd, as fate can swing both ways; you may win a fortune in the lottery, or come up with a marvellous invention the takes the world by storm. In other words, this is a Rune of Karma, which is fair and unbiased, though it may not necessarily reward hard work or good deeds directly. Karma crosses the gap between present and past lives, so you may not understand the reasons behind the work of Wyrd. The simple fact is that with Wyrd, things are completely out of your hands – fate is in the driving seat.

No reversed meaning is feasible when anything and everything are possible, as with a Rune of this nature.

11: Preparing a New Set of Runes

Before using a new set of Runes, lay the whole set on a clean, white cloth and lay your Rune-bag next to the Runes.

Allow yourself to slip into a meditative state and then imagine white light beaming down from the universe and bringing blessings to your Runes. Ask that they will bring good advice and help to those who consult them.

Don't forget to include your Rune-bag in this little ritual.

If someone interferes with your Runes, or indeed with any of your spiritual tools, go through this same process again in order to clear any unwanted vibes or influences from them.

Once your Runes are ready for use, give yourself a couple of trial readings to get them going, then put the Runes in their bag and put them away in a safe place. Store them above head-height, if possible.

12: BEFORE YOU READ YOUR RUNES

While it's always good to have peace and quiet while giving a reading, this isn't always convenient. Professionals often give readings at psychic fairs, fund-raising events, school fêtes, over the radio and on TV. However, it's never a good idea to give readings at a party where people may have too much to drink.

You need to honour your spiritual work, your tools and your spiritual guides. You can give an occasional reading to a sceptic, but for the most part, you will read for those who will trust your gifts and believe that you can help them to gain a little insight.

Making a Start

Close your eyes and ask your spiritual guide, guardian angel or your higher consciousness to give you the guidance you need in order to give a sound reading. Ask for your enquirer to benefit from the reading you give him. If reading for yourself, ask to be given the answers that you need – which may not always be the answers that you'd like to hear.

Give your Rune-bag a shake, while relaxing and leaving the cares of the everyday world behind. Alternatively, put your hand into the bag and stir the Runes around for a while.

If reading for yourself, you may want to focus on a particular matter that you have on your mind, but you could just as easily leave it to the Runes to find their way to the things that are, or will soon become, important to you.

If reading for someone else, tell them to focus on their problems or questions for a few moments before you begin the reading.

As you can see, there is no embargo for reading for yourself, and I would actually recommend that you do give yourself fairly frequent readings while you are in the process of familiarising yourself with the Runes and the various spreads.

Where to Read the Runes?
Tradition says that you should lay out your Runes on a clean, white cloth, but any clear space will do. If you don't have much space in which to work, a tray covered with a cloth or napkin will suffice.

Be Thoughtful.
If reading for someone else, bear in mind that, even if they take a light-hearted approach to you and the reading, they will secretly take what you say to heart. Not everyone shows their feelings, but if you barge ahead without thinking about you are saying, you can really worry or upset your enquirer.

Runes, Tarot cards, astrology, psychism, palmistry and other forms of reading have a weird way of getting to the heart of the matter, and of focusing on the very thing that is closest to you or your enquirer's mind at the time of the reading. In short, the tool you use seeks out the most dramatic or emotive matter in the recent past, present or future, so it's particularly important to take care when giving a reading.

You can choose to read all the Runes in the upright position, or you can include the reversed meanings as well, if any Runes come out upside down.

13: READING THE RUNES

One Rune

You can get an idea of the current situation by giving the Rune-bag a good shake and then picking out one Rune at random. This Rune might describe the present situation, or it may offer advice about the near future.

This is often a good way to make a start in a reading session – a kind of warm-up exercise, and to help relax your client.

Three Runes

Invoke the three Norns of fate by taking three Runes from your Rune-bag, with the first one representing the past, the second representing the present, and the third one for the future.

| PAST | PRESENT | FUTURE |

Past: The background to the current situation.

Present   As things are now.

Future: Possibilities, opportunities, warnings, choices to be made, or matters of fate and destiny.

The Nine Random Runes Layout

Lay a white linen napkin on your table and ask the enquirer to shake the Rune-bag a little. Then let him pick out nine Runes at random. He should gently throw the Runes onto the cloth. Don't try to lay the Runes out in a specific pattern, just read them as they lie.

You begin by reading the pieces that have the Rune symbol showing (i.e. uppermost), leaving those that fell face down for the time being.

Now you have a choice, because you can elect to read the Runes as if they were all in the upright position, or you can decide to read those that fell upright or sideways as upright, and the others as reversed.

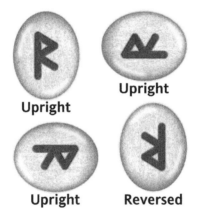

Upright

Upright

Upright

Reversed

Now you can turn over the Runes that fell face down, and these should be considered a guide to the future rather than the present.

The position of the Runes is also important, in that those in the centre of the cloth are at the heart of the enquirer's life, while those that fell around the edge of the cloth are less central to his immediate problem. Those that don't land on the cloth at all are the least important of all.

See how the Runes are grouped and use the "rule of three" to judge if any of the Runes are in a close group of three. These groups may point to something that will soon be happening in the client's life.

Upright and Reversed Readings
Some people only ever read the Runes in an upright position, while others include the reversed meanings when Runes fall upside down when pulled out of the Rune-bag. Whatever you do is right for you, but it isn't necessarily right for someone else, so don't try to impose your beliefs or methods on someone else.

I stress this point because one day some years ago, my wife, Sasha, was invited to give a talk to a Tarot group; while there, she was horrified to hear the bossy organiser of the event loudly insisting that proper Tarot Readers should _only_ ever read the cards in the upright position! I personally agree with Sasha, as we don't mind how people read their cards, Runes or anything else; you should always do what feels right for you.

For my part (and Sasha's), I think that 24 Runes is too small a number to give much of a reading, so adding the reversed meanings and the blank Rune give 49 possible answers, which makes life much easier and more accurate. But, as already stressed here, experiment and find the method that works best for you.

That doesn't mean you have to use a large number of Runes in your readings, it just means that you have more potential interpretations to call upon. It can also be useful when looking at the nature of the people around the enquirer, or looking at the way they are likely to behave. For instance, are they likely to help or harm the enquirer? A reversed Rune can be very useful in revealing the hidden motivations of others.

14: LARGER SPREADS

Past, Present and Future in Detail

Nine Runes give a detailed account to what has been leading up to the present situation, how it is manifesting now, and the potential outcome.

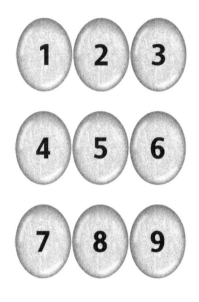

Past: gives a deeper insight into the background of the client's question.

Present: Shows what the client and those around him are doing, along with the general surrounding atmosphere in his life.

Future: How things can change, progress, become a problem and so on. Gives advice about people and circumstances in the future.

The Pyramid Spread

This layout starts from the bottom and works its way upward. The base of the pyramid represents the past, the middle rows are the present leading into the future, and the top Rune is the future.

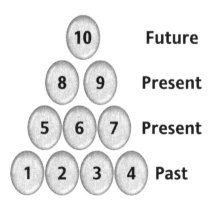

A Column of Seven Runes

This is a simple method that can be very useful when you want some insight and don't have much time to spare. You can lay the Runes in a horizontal line or a vertical one, as follows:

1   The Questioner

2   People or things that are against him

3   People or things that are helpful to him

4   Future events that can be expected

5   Future events that are completely unexpected

6   Suggestions as to the best course of action

7   The eventual outcome

Yggdrasil – The World Tree

This is useful for questions of a spiritual nature, and the reading begins by looking at the first four Runes to discover the background to the question.

1   Why the client is embarking on a period of spiritual development

2   Unknown factors that have already happened

3   The known past

4   Factors that lead from the past to the present

5   The present

6   Inner urges leading to unconscious decisions

7   Known, conscious factors leading to logical decisions

8   Leading to the future

9   Future spiritual development

10   Unexpected outcome

11   Overall outcome

Runic Houses

1.   *The House of Berkano*
Beginnings, fertility, birth, motherhood, growth

2.   *The House of Laguz*
Increase and growth, improving health and energy, developing intuition and ESP, joining something new.

3.   *The House of Daguz*
Sudden changes, dawn of an unexpected new day

4.   *The House of Thurisaz*
Protection from personal attack and from enemies, the strength to resist oppression

5.   *The House of Kaunaz*
Education, inspiration, creativity, artistry

6.   *The House of Hagalaz*
Transformation, metamorphosis, but within the prevailing situation

7.   *The House of Jera*
    Completion, the result, the annual harvest, success, luck

8.   *The House of Algiz*
    Divine guidance and angelic help, along with inner strength and the ability to defend oneself against physical or spiritual attack

The Wheel Spread

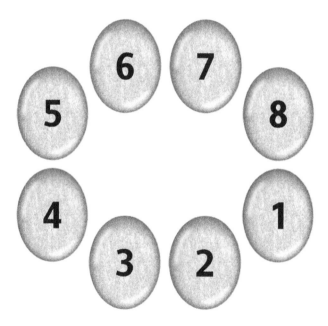

If one of the Runes mentioned in the preceding List of Runic Houses falls anywhere in the positions in this reading, its meaning is emphasised, while a Rune landing in its own house position (for instance, Kaunaz in position 5), it becomes even more important.

15: THE COMPASS LAYOUT

Y ou need to find a large piece of paper for this reading, and draw the image below. Make it about four or five times the size of the image in this book.

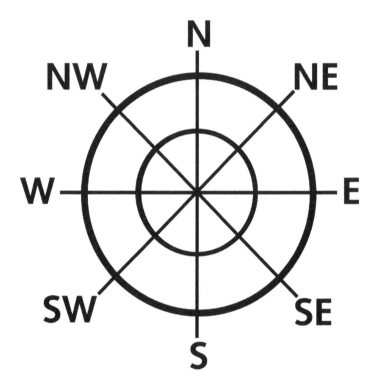

When you wish to give a reading, shake your Rune-bag and take fifteen Runes at random from it.

Throw them gently onto the design

> 1. Turn any Runes face up that landed face down, so that you can see what they are. Keep them in the spot where they landed. If you like using the upright and reversed system, consider any Runes lying sideways as upright. However, if you

wish to ignore reversed meanings, then by all means, read all the Runes as being upright.

2. The Runes in the inner circle talk about things that are close to the enquirer's heart. These will also relate to matters affecting the family, loved ones and domestic life. Health may also be an issue here.

3. The Runes that fall in the outer circle are concerned with more distant matters. These may be work, friends and acquaintances, or relatives who aren't closely related to the enquirer. These Runes could also denote a host of other matters that may not be vitally important, but which are having some kind of effect on his life.

4. Runes that fall outside the outer circle are less important – but the fact that they are in the reading at all means they may become important in the future.

5. You may wish to take note of the compass points, as they can offer additional information. Firstly, they may indicate the direction from which good things or potential troubles are coming. Alternatively, the direction in which people who will become important to the enquirer will be found.

6. A more traditional and less practical way of using the compass directions is to judge any Rune that falls in the north as being difficult. Even a good Rune can have its effects limited if it falls in the north.

7. Any Rune that falls in the south area will be helped by being there, so a "good news" Rune will be even better than it might otherwise have been; similarly, a difficult Rune will not have too bad an influence, or perhaps the difficulty will only be of a short duration.

8. The east represents new people or situations, and some kind of fresh start, while the west is about unfinished business or things that are coming to a conclusion.

What and Where?

Let's suppose that Gebo is in the outer circle, in the north. Gebo talks about giving and receiving presents, affection, kindness, and even kisses. If in a hard position and perhaps also reversed, this would suggest that you are being, or soon will be, used by others and taken advantage of, maybe even in the name of love.

How about Pertho in the south, in the inner circle? This Rune denotes winning, succeeding and solving problems. It could mean educational success or a new enterprise that will work out well. A child may be born to the client, or some other happy event may occur. Needless to say, all this is enhanced if the Rune is in the upright position.

Let's say that Raido is in the east. This could suggest an important journey in that direction, or someone important coming into the questioner's life from the east.

If we put Raido in the west and it is reversed, this could indicate a journey that is linked in some way to the past, a matter that links with things or people to the west, or something that has yet to be concluded.

All this just goes to show how complex and detailed a reading can turn out, if you add in the various extra factors, as per the following summary:

1. The number of Runes used for the reading

2. Upright only, or using reversed as well

3. Inner circle or outer circle, or outside both circles

4. Direction, and therefore the "mood", or added influence that any particular direction can bring

5. The direction in which to look or travel to make something good happen. Alternatively, a direction to avoid going in, and a warning about people who come from a particular direction

And Finally...

You could forget all these complications and simply pick out three Runes, lay them down in the upright position and see what news they bring.

16: CROSSOVER LAYOUTS

The following spreads come from other traditions and divinations, but they may be familiar to you and therefore easy to use.

The Consequences Spread

This handy little spread comes from the Tarot, and it's a useful reading for those times when you have a decision to make, or are looking for advice about the direction you should take.

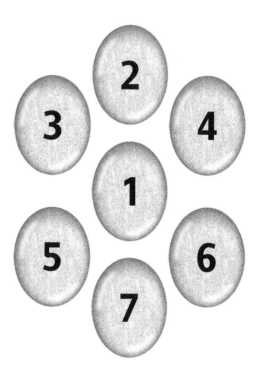

1 The person or situation in question

2 What is for or against the situation

3 Past influences

4   Future influences

5   How others will influence the situation

6   The direction you should take

7   The outcome

The Celtic Cross Spread

This is a version of a well-known Tarot spread.

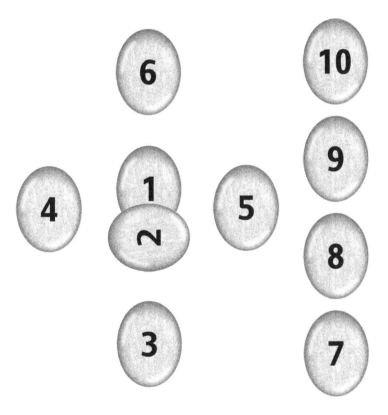

1 The person or situation

2 What is for or against the situation

3 The past

4 The recent past

5 The near future

6 The best one can expect from the situation

7 How you influence others

8 How others influence you

9 Hopes and fears

10 Outcome

The Twelve Astrological Houses Spread

This spread is based on an astrological concept. The first house is on the right, and the sequence runs anticlockwise.

1 The person, situation, the start of something

2 Money, personal possessions, a person's image

3 Siblings, the neighbourhood, communications

4 The home, family and parents (especially mother figures)

5 Children, fun, glamorous goods, holidays, creativity, music

6 Work, health, bosses, employees

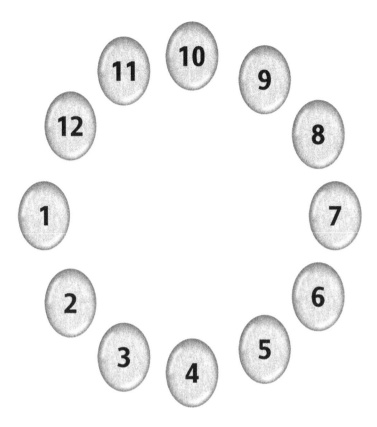

7 Open relationships, open enemies

8 Deep feelings, birth, sex, death, shared resources

9 Legal and educational matters, foreign matters, publishing

10 Status, aims, aspirations, help from people in authority

11 Friends, acquaintances, groups, clubs, societies

12 Hidden factors, self-undoing, artistry, escapism, psychic matters

Feng Shui Spread

The Magic Square design is well-known in China, but you might like to use it from time to time for a change. The place names are short, and therefore easy to interpret.

The Magic Square is so called because the three numbers in any row, column or diagonal always add up to 15.

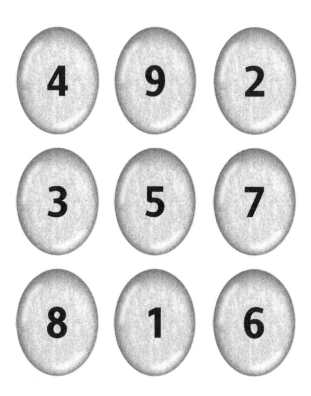

1   Career

2   Relationships

3   Elders

4   Prosperity

5   Health

6   Friends

7   Children

8   Study

9   Recognition or fame

Numerology Spread
This is another quick and easy crossover spread

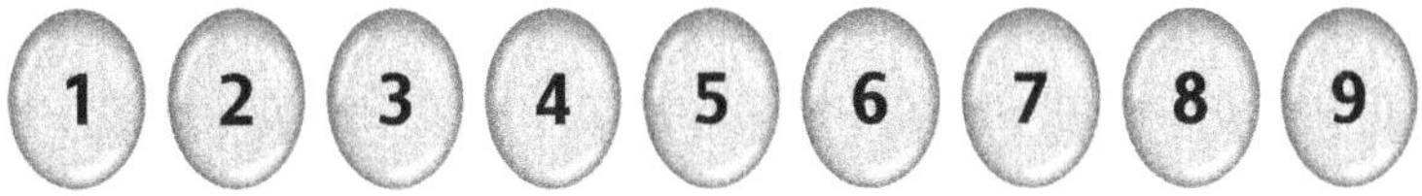

1   Self, ego

2   Relationships, love

3   Creativity

4   Home, personal possessions

5   Communication, travel

6   Duty, family love

7   Spirituality, art, music, relaxation

8   Business, work, success

9   Completion, ending cycles, spiritual journeys

And, Finally...
Need a really quick answer to a question?

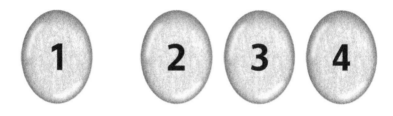

1   The question

2, 3 and 4: describing the answer

17: Magic with the Runes

The Runes have a long history of being used for magical purposes. The difference between divination and magic is that divination is used to *see* what will happen, while magic is used to *make* something happen.

If you regularly practise magic, you will have an altar already set up. If you want to use a Rune or two to enhance your spell casting, choose those that are suited to your specific purpose. For example, if you are casting a spell for someone who wants to have a baby, you could put the Berkano Rune on your altar.

If you need to improve your finances, you could put a Rune of increase or of wealth on the altar. On the other hand, if you are looking for love, success or some other form of happiness, you could select an appropriate Rune for the purpose.

Charging a Rune
Before doing any of this, you may wish to charge your Rune by passing it briefly over some incense smoke or a burning candle; then, imagine white light coming down from the universe and flooding your Rune with a blessing.

Avoid
Never use Runes or any other form of magic to harm others. Such curses will always bounce back on you.

Never try to make someone fall in love with you, or to love you as much as you love them. You'll end up souring the relationship and losing your companion for good.

You can influence others by asking for them to be happier, healthier or wealthier – or even for them to become nicer people, but that's about all. The key principle to keep in mind is to use your magic for positive, beneficial and unselfish ends.

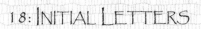

18: INITIAL LETTERS

The letters of the Elder Futhark are close enough to our alphabet for us to follow the Norse tradition of interpreting the names of people by the first letters of their names. This is similar to numerology, except that in numerology, the letters are first converted into numbers.

In Runic mythology, the initial letter of your name shows the kind of luck you will have throughout your life.

OUR ALPHABET	RUNE NAME	RUNE SYMBOL
A	ANSUZ	F
B	BERKANO	ᛒ
C	KAUNAZ	ᚲ
D	DAGUZ	ᛞ
E	EHWAZ	ᛗ
I	ISA / EIHWAZ	ᛁ
F	FEHU	ᚠ
G	GEBO	ᚷ
H	HAGALAZ	ᚺ
I	ISA	ᛁ
J	JERA	ᛃ
K	KAUNAZ	ᚴ
L	LAGUZ	ᛚ

OUR ALPHABET	RUNE NAME	RUNE SYMBOL
M	MANNAZ	ᛗ
N	NAUTHIZ	ᚾ
O	OTHILA	ᛟ
P	PERTHO	ᛈ
Q	KAUNAZ	ᚲ
R	RAIDO	ᚱ
S	SOWELO	ᛋ
T	TIWAZ	ᛏ
U	URUZ	ᚢ
V	FEHU	ᚠ
W	URUZ	ᚹ
X	ALGIZ	ᛉᛁ
Y	ISA or JERA	ᛁ ᛃ
Z	ALGIZ	ᛉ
NG	INGUZ	ᛜ
TH	THURISAZ	ᚦ

The "E" in Eihwaz is pronounced "I", as in "Idea".

Use the list to find the Runes in your own name's first initial letters.

Examples

Kevin	K	KAUNAZ
Sophie	S	SOWELO
John	J	JERA
Anna	A	ANSUZ
Peter	P	PERTHO
Edward	E	EHWAZ
Eileen	E	EIHWAZ
Davis	D	DAGUZ
Thatcher	TH	THURISAZ
Morris	M	MANNAZ
Terry	T	TIWAZ
Carlton	C	KAUNAZ
Nguen	NG	INGUZ

Examples

Sasha Fenton = SF = SOWELO / FEHU

Zambezi Publishing Ltd = ZPL = ALGIZ / PERTHO / LAGUZ

19: PRONUNCIATION

Runes – Pronunciation Table

Opinions differ as to the pronunciation – and spelling – of many Runes' names. The following list presents my version of a typical pronunciation set. Having researched a number of sources, it's clear that, as in the case of the Latin language, the origins of the Runes are so distant and varied in location that no one seems to be absolutely certain of exact pronunciation. Perhaps there isn't one simple set of phonics, as the speech of the Germanic peoples quite possibly differed from other northern communities.

So, my list presents a reasonably standard set of phonics that you can use when discussing the Runic language.

RUNE	OUR EQUIVALENT	PRONUNCIATION
		(as in...)
Fehu	F	(fetch) (who)
Uruz	U	(whose) (look)
Thurisaz	TH	(whose) (list) (as)
Ansuz	A	(and) (snooze)
Raido	R	(ride) (oh!)
Kaunaz	K	(cow) (as)
Gebo	G	(get) (boat)
Wunjo	W	(short "moon") (Joe)

RUNE	OUR EQUIVALENT	PRONUNCIATION
Hagalaz	H	(wag) (wag) (wag)
Nauthiz	N	(cow) (is)
Isa	I	(l-is-t) (at)
Jera	J	(merry) (at)
Eihwaz	EI	(eye) (as)
Pertho	P	(term) (oh!)
Algiz	Z	(therm-al) (is)
Sowelo	S	(sew) (met) (oh!)
Tiwaz	T	(lit) (as)
Berkano	B	(hurl) (darn) (oh!)
Ehwaz	E	(egg) (as)
Mannaz	M	(man) (as)
Laguz	L	(nag) (short "snooze")
Inguz	NG	(ng) (short "snooze")
Othilo	O	(hot) (hill) (oh!)
Dagaz	D	(nag) (as)

CONCLUSION

I hope this brief tour has given you more than just an understanding of the meanings of the fascinating Runes; they were an integral part of the lives of the northern tribes and other nations. In times of old, people had no idea about the causes of "magical" things such as lightning, let alone the power of the seas and other natural events. So, it was essential to create some basic structures and beliefs in order to explain, forecast and cope with the vagaries of nature and the world around them. The godly pantheon that evolved richly displays the imagination and the mindset of these early folk, laying out a unique range of tales and fables that kept people enthralled throughout their lives. We can still experience the stirring emotions brought out by the courageous and hardy actions of all the deities, whether kindly or the opposite.

Closely bound to the mythology is the very practical feature of an alphabet that enabled written records to be produced and passed down through the ages, and, by no means the least attribute of the Runes, we have the wonderful ability of divination for revealing the future and making our lives that much safer and more interesting.

Use the Runes for yourself, cast them for your family and friends, and you'll find that the more you use them, the better you'll become at giving accurate readings, earning you the same level of respect that Readers had in ancient times. What could be more satisfying than being able to help yourself and other people through difficult times? Buy or make yourself a Rune set today, and get started!

INDEX

A

Aesir 26, 34, 40
Aett, Freya's 5
AETT, FREYA'S 42
AETT, HAGALAZ'S 42
Aett, Hagall's 5
Aett, Tyr's 5
AETT, TYR'S 42
Alfheim 39
altar 126
Armageddon 65
Asgard 26, 39, 40, 56
ash tree 54
Asynjur 40
Audhumla 49, 51
Auroch 51

B

Baldur 36, 40
Bifrost 38, 56
boar 88
Bohemia 20

C

Cleansing 44
Column of Seven Runes 107

D

Dishonoured Dead 40
Draupnir 58

E

Elder Futhark 128
elves, dark 39
elves, fair 39

Etruscans 20

F
Fenris Wolf 36, 39, 79
Frey 36, 39, 49
Freya 27, 36, 39, 49
Frigga 36, 40, 60
Futhark 48
FUTHARK 8

G
German lands 20
Germania 20, 21
giants 38
Ginnungagap 38
Gleipnir 39
god Rune 54
golden boar 88
Gullinbursti 88

H
Hagal 64
Havamal 26
Heimdall 36, 56, 64, 65, 74
Hel 40
Helheim 40
Hengist 82
Hodur 36
Horsa 82
horse 82
Hugin 54
Hvergelmir 38

I
Icelandic Rune Poem 86

Ing 88
Invocation to Odin 7
Iving 38

J
Jotunheim 30, 38
Jotuns 38

K
Kaunaz 56
Kent 82

L
Loki 36, 40

M
Magic Square 122
Mercury 54
middle earth 38
Midgard 38
Midgard Serpent 38
Mimir's Well of Wisdom 38
Munin 54
Muspelheim 39

N
Nidhog 38, 67
Niflheim 30, 38, 67
Nine Worlds 36
Njord 26, 36, 39, 49, 86
Norn 51, 69
Norns 34
Norse Runes 5

O
Odin 7, 36
owl 56

P
pantheon 34
Pluto 53
Poetic Edda 26

R
Ragnarok 27, 36, 39, 56
Rainbow Bridge 36, 56, 65, 74
Raunen 20
ravens 54
retrograde 54
Reversed Readings 104
Ruenes 20
Runa 20
Rúnatal 26
Rune 20
Rune cards 44
Rune Poem 26
Runic Houses 109

S
Scandinavia 20
Skuld 34
Sleipnir 30, 82
Slovakia 20
Spread, Celtic Cross 119
Spread, Consequences 118
Spread, Feng Shui 122
Spread, Numerology 123
Spread, Pyramid 106
Spread, Twelve Astrological Houses 120

Spread, Wheel 110
Surt 39
Swartalfheim 39

T
Tacitus 20
Thor 36, 53, 92
Thor's hammer 51
Three Runes 102
Three Sisters 34
Thursday 53
Thursur giants 53
Tyr 36

U
Urd 30, 34, 51
Uruz 51

V
Valhalla 40
Valkyries 74
Vanaheim 26, 36, 39
Vanir 26, 34, 36
Vanir gods 39
Ve 38
Verdandi 34, 69
Vikings 40
Vili 38

W
war god 79
Wave Maidens 36
World Tree 27
Wulfila, Bishop 20
Wyrd 30, 34, 94

Y
yew tree 72
Yggdrasil 7, 27, 30, 36, 54, 108
Ymir 38, 49

Zambezi Publishing Ltd

We hope you have enjoyed reading this book. The Zambezi range of books includes titles by top level, internationally acknowledged authors on fresh, thought-provoking viewpoints in your favourite subjects. A common thread with all our books is the easy accessibility of content; we have no sleep-inducing tomes, just down-to-earth, easily digestible, credible books.

~~~~~

Please visit our website (www.zampub.com) to browse our full range of Lifestyle and Mind, Body & Spirit (MB&S) titles, and to discover what might spark your interest next...

~~~~~

For an equally absorbing range of non-MB&S titles and details of all our ebooks, visit our sister website, www.stelliumpub.com

Lightning Source UK Ltd.
Milton Keynes UK
UKOW06f1057260216

269159UK00008B/124/P